SOCIAL AND ECONOMIC WELL-BEING



# When Autonomous Vehicles Are Hacked, Who Is Liable?

Zev Winkelman, Maya Buenaventura, James M. Anderson,
Nahom M. Beyene, Pavan Katkar, Gregory Cyril Baumann

For more information on this publication, visit www.rand.org/t/RR2654

**Library of Congress Cataloging-in-Publication Data** is available for this publication.
ISBN: 978-1-9774-0323-0

Published by the RAND Corporation, Santa Monica, Calif.


*Cover: Adobe Stock/Production Perig.*

# Preface

This report examines the civil liability implications that would flow from hackers commandeering or hacking autonomous vehicles (AVs) and using them to cause harm. Thanks to AVs, roles and civil legal response may shift among manufacturers, component makers, dealers, and owners (be they individual or fleet owners). Factor in the likelihood that hackers will attack AVs, and it becomes prudent to begin mapping the kind of damages that could arise—and who may face claims for damages. The RAND Institute for Civil Justice funded this work. Participants in the auto industry and the technology field, insurers, legal professionals, and potential owners of driverless cars will find value in this discussion of the liability implications of hackers attacking AVs.

## RAND Institute for Civil Justice

The RAND Institute for Civil Justice (ICJ) is dedicated to improving the civil justice system by supplying policymakers and the public with rigorous and nonpartisan research. Its studies identify trends in litigation and inform policy choices concerning liability, compensation, regulation, risk management, and insurance. The Institute builds on a long tradition of RAND Corporation research characterized by an interdisciplinary, empirical approach to public policy issues and rigorous standards of quality, objectivity, and independence. ICJ research is supported by pooled grants from a range of sources, including corporations, trade and professional associations, individuals, government agencies, and private foundations. All its reports are subject to peer review and disseminated widely to policymakers, practitioners in law and business, other researchers, and the public. The ICJ is part of the Justice Policy Program within the RAND Social and Economic Well-Being Division. The program focuses on such topics as access to justice, policing, corrections, drug policy, and court system reform, as well as other policy concerns pertaining to public safety and criminal and civil justice. For more information, email justicepolicy@rand.org.

## RAND Ventures

The RAND Corporation is a research organization that develops solutions to public policy challenges to help make communities throughout the world safer and more secure, healthier and more prosperous. RAND is nonprofit, nonpartisan, and committed to the public interest.

RAND Ventures is a vehicle for investing in policy solutions. Philanthropic contributions support our ability to take the long view, tackle tough and often-controversial topics, and share our findings in innovative and compelling ways. RAND's research findings and recommendations are based on data and evidence, and therefore do not necessarily reflect the policy preferences or interests of its clients, donors, or supporters.

Funding for this venture was provided by gifts from RAND supporters and income from operations.

# Contents

# Figures and Tables

## Figures



## Tables

# Summary

The arrival of autonomous vehicles (AVs) on our roads will require policymakers, industry, and the public to adapt to the risk of computer hackers attacking these vehicles. Given AVs' potential to cause physical damage when commandeered and the likelihood of other adverse consequences if hacked, the RAND Institute for Civil Justice undertook an exploration of the civil liability issues around likely scenarios involving hacked driverless cars.

To help parties anticipate coming changes, we conducted a review of the research on the properties of AVs and the driving environment. Similarly, we studied AVs' potential vulnerabilities to hackers and the types of damage that could result from exploitation of those vulnerabilities. We considered how models of vehicle ownership and use might change and how roles and responsibilities may shift among participants in the AV economy. Finally, we married an analysis of existing theories of civil liability (relevant to the fields of both computer hacking and conventional vehicles) to four scenarios to help decisionmakers and other interested parties understand where policy responses may be needed.

This report envisions four scenarios to aid in understanding how liability may play out:

- a ransomware attack
- a hacked vehicle damaging government property
- hacks on a connected roadway that cause damage
- theft of information through car hacking.

Our analysis of those scenarios provided insight into ways that civil liability will likely exist for participants in the AV economy. In particular, we examined liability issues pertaining to AV manufacturers, software and component makers, owners and operators of AVs, and state and federal governments.

We identified several preliminary findings of particular interest relevant to those parties. First, existing civil liability law will likely be sufficiently flexible to adapt to most hacked AV liability claims. There is no immediate necessity for Congress or state legislatures to pass statutes to address this set of risks. However, further research on the extent to which cyberattacks on AVs are covered by existing automobile and commercial insurance policies would be helpful. Similarly, research on the ability of the insurance system to compensate for a large-scale cyberattack would be helpful. Exclusions for acts of war in many insurance policies, the difficulties in determining the attackers, and the potential magnitude of the damages may create challenges to the existing liability system.

AV manufacturers, manufacturers and designers of component parts and software, and distributors of AVs may face civil liability for criminal hacks on AVs under well-established legal precedent.

Product liability laws—along with warranty law and state and federal privacy laws—are the most relevant body of law. Because of the role of foreseeability in determinations of liability for the criminal acts of a third party (like hacking), the issue of prior exploitation of a vulnerability of a component part or system in an AV will likely play an important role in liability determinations. Cost-benefit analysis of possible precautions that could have averted a particular attack will also play an important role.

Cost-benefit and foreseeability analyses thus will influence legal analysis of responsibility for damages from cyberattacks. These cost-benefit analyses will require courts and juries to become familiar with the technology at issue, most likely through the use of experts. Manufacturers of vehicles and component parts will need to stay abreast of attacks on AVs and take any necessary precautions to avoid similar attacks if they wish to avoid liability.

Users of AVs may also face liability for cyberattacks if, for example, they reject an important security update, allowing a hacker to take control of the AV and steer it into another vehicle. Clarifying automobile insurance coverages for these events would also be useful.

Government agencies may be potential defendants in civil lawsuits that arise out of incidents involving unsafe infrastructure. Although sovereign immunity may protect these agencies in some situations, immunity may not apply as they undertake ministerial tasks, such as road maintenance. Thus, after AVs and supporting infrastructure develop, government agencies will be more likely to be held civilly liable if their negligence provides an attacker an opportunity to cause a crash. In addition, significant municipal and state engagement in infrastructure development will be necessary if the connected vehicle environment relies on communications between AVs and roadside infrastructure. This would open the door for negligence claims against state and local authorities.

In light of these findings, policymakers should consider the following questions:

- Should statutes be used to clarify legal responsibility for various harms that can be anticipated to arise from hacked AVs, instead of relying on the more-flexible common-law process?
- How should governmental and judicial expertise in technologies that will prevent cyberattacks be developed and maintained?
- What regulations might be appropriate to prevent or mitigate harms that would arise from hacked AVs causing damage?

The realization of the societal benefits of AVs would benefit from the following actions:

- developing a framework for measuring the cybersecurity and safety of AVs[1]

---

1 See, e.g., Fraade-Blanar et al., 2018.

- better understanding insurance coverages for cyberattacks on AVs, both for commercial and consumer policies, to determine who will bear the costs of such attacks
- better understanding who would bear the costs in case of a large-scale cyberattack on AVs and whether a reinsurance backstop would be useful.

# Acknowledgments

We would like to acknowledge the many participants in numerous conferences that have directly and indirectly shaped our thinking on these topics. In particular, we would like to acknowledge Karlyn Stanley and Ellen Partridge for organizing the legal breakout sessions at the 2016, 2017, and 2018 Automated Vehicles Symposiums. We also thank Marjory Blumenthal and Dorothy Glancy for their careful reviews of this report.

## Abbreviations

| | |
|---|---|
| Auto-ISAC | Automotive Information Sharing and Analysis Center |
| AV | autonomous vehicle |
| CAN | controller area network |
| CPS | cyber-physical system |
| DHS S&T | U.S. Department of Homeland Security Science and Technology Directorate |
| DMV | Department of Motor Vehicles |
| DoS | denial of service |
| DOT | U.S. Department of Transportation |
| DSRC | dedicated short-range communication |
| ECU | electronic control unit |
| GDPR | European Union General Data Protection Regulation |
| GM | General Motors |
| GPS | Global Positioning System |
| LiDAR | light detection and ranging |
| mph | miles per hour |

| | |
|---|---|
| NHTSA | National Highway Traffic Safety Administration |
| NIST | National Institute of Standards and Technology |
| OBD-II | onboard diagnostics–II |
| SAE | Society of Automotive Engineers |
| UCC | Uniform Commercial Code |
| V2I | vehicle-to-infrastructure |
| V2V | vehicle-to-vehicle |
| V2X | vehicle-to-X [where X represents anything that is not a vehicle or infrastructure element] |

CHAPTER ONE

# Introduction—Understanding the Context

It is simple to imagine the potential benefits of self-driving cars: Increased mobility for people who cannot drive, the promise of safer roadways, and hours of driving time dedicated to more-productive uses are among potential benefits.[1] It is also easy, however, to envision the danger and damage that they could cause if hackers were to commandeer these fast, heavy artificial intelligences on wheels. Even less dramatic consequences of hacking (e.g., stealing the personal information of a passenger or attacking using ransomware) can be problematic.

We already understand the damage that conventional vehicles can cause when put to ill use: eight dead in terrorist ramming attacks in New York City (Mueller, Rashbaum, and Baker, 2017); vehicles driven through storefronts in "crash and grab" robberies, suicide car bombs. Hackers could turn self-driving cars, referred to in this report as *autonomous vehicles* (AVs),[2] into tools of similar mayhem—and invent new forms of remote-controlled mischief. That potential indicates the need for policies that anticipate the damage that AV hackers could cause. This report explores the liability implications of hacked cars causing

---

[1] See, generally, Anderson et al., 2016.

[2] Throughout this report, we use the terms *self-driving cars*, *highly automated vehicles*, and *autonomous vehicles* interchangeably. While *highly automated vehicles* may be the most precise formulation, most audiences do not meaningfully distinguish among the terms.

The U.S. Department of Transportation's (DOT's) Federal Automated Vehicles Policy uses the Society of Automotive Engineers (SAE) International's six levels of vehicle automation to describe the capabilities of driverless cars. SAE describes levels of automation from 0–5, with 0 having no automation. Levels 4 and 5 describe vehicles that are designed to handle all aspects of driving under certain conditions without human intervention.

damage. It employs plausible scenarios to analyze which parties might face liability and examines the legal theories that may apply.

For the purposes of this report, we are interested in vehicles that are capable of being hacked. Given the subject of the report, the primary criteria of relevance is not a particular level of driving function or operational design domain but the ability and likelihood of being hacked. Although the most alarming scenarios that involve commandeered vehicles would most likely involve vehicle systems of SAE levels 3 or greater, vehicles with level 1 or 2 systems could cause serious harm under certain scenarios.[3]

We define *hacking* as a deliberate attempt by a nonauthorized user to affect the vehicle in some material way. This includes, most alarmingly, commandeering the vehicle, but also attempting to partly control it, materially misleading the relevant artificial intelligence, or using ransomware. It also includes efforts to obtain personal or other data from the vehicle or system. It excludes inadvertent errors in the software code that may lead to a crash or other non-deliberate actions, mechanical failures, or malfunctions.

The expected widespread use of AVs and the near certainty that hackers will take an interest in them suggests many questions:

- What might motivate hackers to commandeer an AV?
- What avenues of attack could hackers use to take over an AV?
- What harm could a hacked AV cause?
- Who (other than the hackers) could be held responsible for those harms?
- What legal theories might support findings of liability?
- How might policymakers react to this new technology and the litigation it may spawn?

How those questions are answered will inform the development of an entire industry, potentially bearing on billions of dollars of investment and millions of people's lives. Likewise, policymakers' approach

---

[3] While conventional fully human-operated vehicles can be hacked under certain circumstances, the requirement of physical proximity to the vehicle and the vehicle's lack of connectivity make this risk smaller.

to AVs and the risk that they will be hacked will affect how fast their benefits spread—and what costs society deems acceptable. Many parties will be affected by the legal framework that develops around self-driving cars and thus may benefit from our analysis: individual car owners, fleet owners, vehicle manufacturers, those who perform maintenance on AVs, and AV software makers and component makers, among others. Behind many of those parties, investors will be seeking to profit from a future of ubiquitous AVs. Regulators, legislators, judges, insurers, attorneys for both plaintiffs and defendants, and legal academics will be confronted with novel problems and opportunities to guide future policies.

This analysis puts a spotlight on some of the tensions that will accompany the adoption of AVs. These vehicles combine existing cars' physical safety systems with cybersecurity systems that are notoriously bad at keeping attackers out. Conventional vehicles are highly regulated, engineered for safety, and backed by processes with decades of scientific rigor. With cybersecurity, on the other hand, we are still at the dawn of a new era. The significant uncertainty in how to model the risk of hacking, and the complexity and vulnerability of the many systems envisioned in a future of AVs, merit pause. The potential benefits of AVs are many and may ultimately outweigh new risks. But those risks will exist.

A technology's net benefit can only be determined by measuring whether it is being used for good or ill—but measuring costs and benefits can be extremely difficult. This is even more difficult when measurement depends on speculative predictions about future development of an emerging technology. This exploration is designed to help interested parties anticipate the civil liability implications of the coming era of AVs, as well as potential policy responses.

Simultaneously, of course, engineers and researchers are hard at work devising technical means to minimize the likelihood of successful cyberattacks on AVs. The specific content of these efforts is outside the scope of this report. Although we are hopeful that these efforts may make the subject of this report moot, the history of cybersecurity and the regular occurrence of successful attacks suggest that substantial risk remains.

CHAPTER TWO

# Autonomous Vehicles and Future Roadways

To analyze the liability implications of hacked cars, one must understand AVs and the connected transportation world they will inhabit. AVs and the infrastructure around them are one type of *cyber-physical system* (CPS), a term that describes the connection of physical products to computer networks. The research on CPSs is maturing, but a framework on how to safely and securely deploy such technologies has yet to emerge.

We must layer over that maturing technology the uncertainty as to how hacking may affect CPSs. A working group of the National Institute of Standards and Technology (NIST) is developing a framework to illustrate the many dimensions involved in the cyber protection, or assurance, of CPSs.[1] At the widest scope, these CPSs will encompass the developing internet of things, where devices of all kinds, not just cars, will be connected to computer systems. Thus, our discussion of the liability implications of AVs may inform other facets of the internet of things. Our analysis in Chapter Five of this report will use the NIST framework to analyze how the roles of manufacturers, AV owners, and others in the ecosystem will change as AVs become widespread.

While existing vehicles incorporate electronic control units (ECUs) and computers that could be hacked, their physical and electronic separation from the internet protects them. However, nearly

---

[1] See NIST, 2018. Of course, numerous other government agencies, including the U.S. Department of Homeland Security and the U.S. Department of Defense, have also been working on identifying and remediating cybersecurity vulnerabilities. We focus on the NIST framework because we found it most useful for thinking about this category of cyberthreats.

every vision of highly automated vehicles relies on the vehicles electronically connecting to other vehicles and infrastructure. These connections introduce vulnerabilities.

AVs connect to CPSs in three potential ways: vehicle-to-vehicle (V2V), vehicle-to-infrastructure (V2I), and vehicle-to-*X* (V2X), where *X* represents any other type of connection an AV may use. V2V connections are thought important because they will enable AVs to rapidly respond to other cars on the road, although both the need for this and the precise form of the connectivity remains uncertain. V2I connections will allow AVs to plan their routes based on information from such sources as connected roadways, parking areas, and fuel or charging stations. V2X connections include connections to manufacturers for software updates and repairs and connections to entertainment systems or smartphones.

Hackers can be expected to test both AVs and the systems they connect to. To explore the liability implications of those hacks, we need to examine the cyber vulnerabilities of both cars and the connected road ecosystem they will drive in.

## What Is an Autonomous Vehicle, and How Does It Work?

A fully autonomous vehicle uses onboard sensors and computers to understand its surroundings, plan its actions, and execute those plans to reach a destination. To survey the plausible cyberattacks on AVs, we reviewed the research literature on attacks against some of the most important components of an AV. Those components include

- sensors
- sensor/actuator control (a computer that acts as a decision engine, analyzing sensor input and sending signals to mechanisms that control the car)
- wireless access to computer systems (which allows communication with other AVs, connected roadways, and authorized networks, such as the manufacturer's)

- autopilot and navigator elements to control vehicle movement and direction.

A diagram illustrating the most important components of AVs is shown in Figure 2.1.

The sensors collect data about the car's surroundings[2] and pass those data to the decision engine (sensor/actuator control), a computer that combines those data with any incoming information from networks, such as from connected roadways or other vehicles. The decision engine analyzes all those data and decides what action to take. The sensor/actuator control sends a corresponding instruction to the appropriate component. For example, the sensor notifies the decision engine that there is an obstacle in front of the car. The decision engine processes that information, decides to hit the brakes, and sends, say, the "apply brakes" instruction to the braking system to halt the car. All

**Figure 2.1**
**Diagram of Autonomous Vehicle Components**

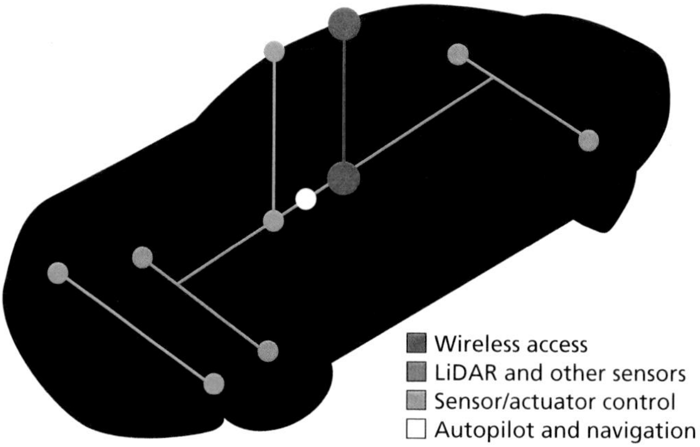


SOURCE: Adapted from Wyglinski et al. (2013, p. 84).
NOTE: LiDAR = light detection and ranging.

---

[2] Most testing models use one or more LiDAR sensors, with the largest exception being Tesla, which has developed limited autonomy based on camera sensors and has publicly indicated that it plans to develop self-driving capabilities without LiDAR.

these systems together form the vulnerable area, or attack surface, of the AV ecosystem that hackers may seek to exploit.

## The Ecosystem of Autonomous Vehicles

To better understand AVs' cyber vulnerabilities, we begin by sketching out a stylized ecosystem in which AVs are likely to operate (Figure 2.2).

As shown in the figure, the ecosystem has four components: production, operation and maintenance, smart infrastructure, and insurance and regulation. Each of these components is explained in detail below.

**Figure 2.2**
**Ecosystem of Autonomous Vehicles**

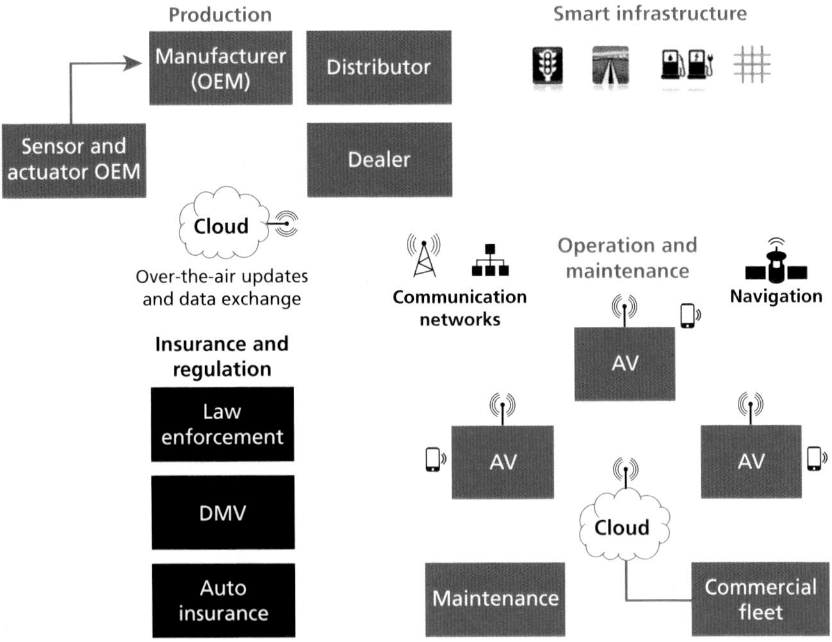


NOTES: DMV = Department of Motor Vehicles; OEM = original equipment manufacturer.

## Production

Five main categories of entities are likely to have physical or remote access to an AV that would permit hacks: manufacturers (of the AV or its original equipment), sensor and actuator makers, distributors, dealers, and aftermarket companies. We have seen this kind of access already—for example, Tesla delivers over-the-air software updates to its cars (Acker and Beaton, 2016). This kind of remote access creates a vulnerability that hackers may attempt to exploit (Ring, 2015). Similarly, if distributors, dealers, and aftermarket sellers of modifications connect to AVs, hackers could target those channels. Lastly, hackers might attempt to exploit vulnerabilities in AV sensors or actuators.

## Operation and Maintenance

### *Operation*

AVs will likely communicate with devices, such as mobile phones, as well as smart infrastructure, such as connected roadways, to improve convenience, safety, and efficiency. In V2V communication, AVs may connect to each other for safety or for the purposes of cooperative driving, also known as *platooning*.[3]

Smartphones can be used to control car entertainment and information systems and, in some cases, the car itself (Lee, An, and Shin, 2011). Tesla, for example, has enabled the use of cell phones to summon vehicles from parking lots. Maps or navigation service providers will also communicate with the AV to provide directions.

Furthermore, a fleet of AVs can be managed remotely using cloud computing services. This arrangement is called a vehicular cloud (Gerla et al., 2014). Vehicular clouds will likely have the capability to provide all the essential services that an AV may need, such as routing, spectrum sharing, and protection against cyberattacks (Gerla et al., 2014). In most cases, the vehicular cloud will be owned and operated by third-

---

[3] Platooning aims to increase the safety and efficiency of traffic on the road by enabling AVs to form "a flexible platoon over a couple of lanes with a short inter-vehicle distance while performing [operations such as] lane changing, merging, and leaving the platoon" (Kato et al., 2002, p. 155). Platooning can substantially increase fuel economy and increase the capacity of a given amount of road space.

party cloud providers, which may introduce new vulnerabilities and complicate the attribution of fault.

Some models of AV operation depend on the possibility of operating the vehicles remotely, from a central control station.[4] While this may be a sensible way of helping vehicles negotiate unusual situations, this capability also offers the potential for hacking.

### *Maintenance*

AV mechanics, both human and, potentially, automated, will likely have physical or remote access to address any problems an AV may encounter (You, Krage, and Jalics, 2005). With AVs, we can anticipate hardware maintenance and software maintenance. Hardware maintenance is the typical kind of work conducted today at repair facilities, such as changing oil and fixing broken tail lamps. It may also include fixing (and cleaning) the LiDAR or other sensors and ECUs. Software maintenance could include updating the firmware or software of the various computational and digital components of the AV. Software updates could either be done via over-the-air updates or by plugging in the AV at an authorized maintenance service provider.

### Smart Infrastructure

To take full advantage of an AV's capacity for safety and smoother traffic, connected roadways and other forms of smart infrastructure may develop. This smart infrastructure could monitor and analyze information through sensors and communicate with vehicles to inform their driving decisions. For example, smart infrastructure could monitor the density of vehicles on a freeway; if traffic is bad, the infrastructure can tell AVs to seek other routes.

---

[4] The California DMV regulations explicitly discuss this. See California Code of Regulations, Title 13, Division 1, Chapter 1, Article 3.7 ("Testing of Autonomous Vehicles"), Section 227 (n):

> "Remote operator" is a natural person who: possesses the proper class of license for the type of test vehicle being operated; is not seated in the driver's seat of the vehicle; engages and monitors the autonomous vehicle; is able to communicate with occupants in the vehicle through a communication link. A remote operator may also have the ability to perform the dynamic driving task for the vehicle or cause the vehicle to achieve a minimal risk condition.

Another form of smart infrastructure would be charging stations for electric vehicles that can communicate with AVs to manage which cars charge where and when. For example, an electric AV running out of power may seek out a nearby charging station that has free power ports. Also, in the process of charging, the AV may communicate via a physical connection with the power ports. One scenario involving the power grid illustrates an interesting aspect of the V2I connection. In such interactions, a fleet of electric vehicles could transmit energy back into the smart electric grid (Su et al., 2012). In this way, the power grid could take advantage of the battery capacity of stationary vehicles to meet peak demand.

These smart infrastructure illustrations involve corresponding hacking vulnerabilities. V2I connections expand the list of potential defendants subject to lawsuits should hackers commandeer vehicles (or fleets of vehicles) and use them to destroy things.

### Insurance and Regulation

Insurance companies might interact with AVs. For example, they may conduct pre-insurance inspections either physically or remotely before insuring an AV. This could create a potentially vulnerable connection. Insurers may also continuously monitor the location and driving behavior of the automated driving system.

State DMVs and state departments of transportation may also connect to AVs. In some states, the registration process requires a physical inspection of a vehicle. It is plausible that a similar, perhaps remotely conducted, inspection may be possible for AVs. This also implies a system and connection that could be hacked. Law enforcement agencies may seek to force installation of a "kill switch" on AVs that could disable them to neutralize dangers or prevent criminals from escaping (Szwed, 1999). More-mundane applications may find law enforcement seeking to route AVs around road construction, parades, or other traffic disruptions.

CHAPTER THREE

# How Can Hackers Exploit Autonomous Vehicles?

Because computers are susceptible to cyberattacks, it is not surprising that AVs are susceptible to cyberattacks as well (Keen Security Lab of Tencent, 2016). This chapter discusses the methods that hackers could use to commandeer AVs. The dangers springing from a car being hacked are compounded when one thinks of a fleet of AVs communicating with each other as a network of computers in motion. That makes AVs potentially susceptible to attacks that both scale up and scale out in terms of the damage they could cause.

By *scaling up*, we mean that attackers will have the opportunity to maximize the impact of their actions. In a recent hack of the financial system, attackers were able to make off with $81 million (Gopalakrishnan and Mogato, 2016). A single vehicle crash took out a $60 million fighter jet (Laurendeau and Barbeau, 2006). When attackers gain precise control over even a single moving vehicle, the damages can be quite large.

*Scaling out* refers to a different phenomenon. The flaws in AV systems that are exploited in an attack are likely duplicated widely in both software and hardware. Therefore, once discovered, they can significantly amplify the consequences. In some cases, the components that get hacked might not be directly related to autonomy or connectivity—for example, hacking wireless keys to unlock doors (Greenberg, 2016a; Greenberg, 2016b). In other cases, connectivity features, such as the ability to monitor or summon a car through one's smartphone, might be exploited (Adams, 2016; Kelion, 2016). Of greatest concern are deeply rooted flaws in the hardware that might be widely replicated, difficult to patch, and enablers of full-system compromises (Whittaker, 2016).

We found three main avenues that a hacker could use to take control of AVs. For a discussion of current research on cyber exploits against AVs, see Appendix A.

## Hacking the Autonomous Vehicle by Exploiting Software Vulnerabilities

A malicious actor can get unauthorized access to the AV by hacking one of the many electronic components of the vehicle. The electronic components that are known to have been hacked in the past include the information-entertainment system (Miller and Valasek, undated), Bluetooth (Dunning, 2010), and cellular network connectivity (Wright, 2011).

## Physically Hacking the Autonomous Vehicle by Plugging in a Malicious Device

Koscher et al. (2010) have shown that, by plugging a laptop computer into the onboard diagnostics–II (OBD-II) port, they could access the core part of a vehicle's internal network (called the controller area network [CAN]). Once an attacker gets unauthorized access to the CAN, there are many different attacks a hacker can launch. (Tables A.1, A.2, and A.3 in Appendix A describe the kinds of attacks in detail.)

## Hacking the Components of the Autonomous Vehicle Ecosystem

In the AV ecosystem, V2I and V2V communications can be exploited to launch cyberattacks (Sumra et al., 2011). V2I and V2V communications may be carried out using the dedicated short-range communication (DSRC) protocol, which allows short- to mid-range wireless communications, although it is difficult to forecast what protocol will be widely accepted or even whether this band of the spectrum may be reallocated. Some DSRC protocols, however, are known to be vulnerable to various types of cyberattacks, including denial of service (DoS) attacks, Global Positioning System (GPS) spoofing, repudiation, and privacy losses due to location tracking (Laurendeau and Barbeau, 2006). 5G, one means of enabling V2X communications, may be similarly vulnerable because it relies on some of the same operational concepts. Cloud-based processing and data storage offer another set of vulnerabilities. The particular vulnerabilities of each means of communicating with the vehicle will vary, but each channel of communication has the potential to create vulnerabilities.

Examples of hacks on the AV ecosystem could include cyber exploits aimed at electric-car charging stations that seek unauthorized access to AVs being recharged. Similarly, diagnostics and maintenance stations could be compromised and used as an avenue of attack.

Existing research also discusses attacks that compromise the over-the-air software update mechanisms used by AV manufacturers (Sampath et al., 2007). If this mechanism is compromised, then all AVs receiving those updates will be left vulnerable to exploitation. This wide vulnerability allows scaling out of the cars vulnerable to hacks—and the potential real-world damage they could cause.

It is also plausible that attackers could compromise the supply chain of AVs and their parts or take advantage of a *zero-day* vulnerability, a flaw that is built into software and whose discovery allows no time for attack prevention. Because such parts will be an essential component of the AV, every AV would be vulnerable—a potent example of scaling out.

With these avenues of cyberattack in mind, what types of attacks are plausible?

## What Types of Attacks Are Plausible?

Based on the different modes of attacks discussed in the literature, we identified four broad flavors of plausible hacks on AVs. Given the evolving nature of these systems and hackers' adaptations to those changes, it is difficult to identify all of the plausible exploits.

### Disabling Attacks

The literature discusses many kinds of attacks, such as turning the engine off, reconfiguring the fire-timing of the cylinders of a gas or diesel engine to make it stumble, constantly activating the ignition lock, and others (see Appendix A). All of these attacks disable one or more of an AV's systems. The real-world damage resulting from a disabling attack would depend on its timing. If a hacker switches off the ignition while a car is stationary in a parking stall, it is likely not a problem to anyone but the inconvenienced driver. If the car is navigating a city when the attack hits, the potential for damage grows. That variability illustrates the range of scenarios that will need to be explored in assessing the implications of hacked AVs.

### Overprovision of Services Attacks

An overprovision of services attack takes the opposite approach of a disabling attack. It makes the AV provide a service or take an action when no service was requested or any action warranted. Examples of this kind of attack include speeding, braking or not braking, and steering or not steering (see Table 3.1). One comparable analogy to this kind of attack is a DoS attack on a website. In such an attack, millions of service requests are sent to the server with the intention of overwhelming that server so that it is unable to respond to any request. The damages resulting from these kinds of attacks are also dependent on time and location.

### Data Manipulation Attacks

Data manipulation attacks describe exploits that feed corrupt data to the components of the AV. This can lead the components to cause the AV to take no action when action actually is needed or take an action when it is not needed. For example, the attacker could compromise the LiDAR unit of the AV and selectively erase the data in such a way that the AV could be tricked into believing that there was no obstacle in the path of its travel. That could trick it into failing to brake or swerve to avoid crashing into the obstacle. Manipulation of data can take the form of selectively erasing, corrupting, or falsely augmenting data (see the scenarios discussed in Chapter Seven). Similarly, *data poisoning*—

tampering with training data or even with physical signs[1]—in subtle ways could introduce risks.

### Data Theft

Stealing data about a user's travel patterns, eavesdropping on a user's conversations using stock cabin microphones, and similar exploits could be grouped into this type of attack. The AV itself does not furnish the only attack surface for hackers, however. The data centers of the AV manufacturers, component makers, insurers, or DMVs could be compromised, and all information about the AVs in operation could be stolen. In most cases, these kinds of attacks result in loss of privacy. For example, when Target and Equifax were hacked and all of their credit card information was compromised, the result was a massive loss of customer privacy (Riley et al., 2014; Woolley, 2017). It is plausible that attackers could target the servers to which AVs connect.

In many cases, automakers will be using third-party cloud providers to host relevant software and data. These third parties would then become stakeholders and potential defendants.

## Effects of Various Hacks

Table 3.1 supplements the preceding discussion by detailing how hacks on various components of an AV might affect car performance or function. The last four columns describe what kinds of effects are possible if one of the four broad types of attacks is carried out on one of the important control units of an AV.

We have established the plausibility of hackers commandeering AVs and discussed in a preliminary way the potential for resultant physical and economic damages. The next chapter will illustrate in greater detail the damage that these cyber exploits could cause in the real world. In subsequent chapters, we will examine how hacks and their harms may affect the liability of makers, owners, and operators of AVs.

---

[1] For an example of data poisoning, see Sitawarin et al., 2018.

**Table 3.1**
**Hacks on Autonomous Vehicle Components and Their Results**

| Function/ Control Unit | Hack on Component | | Hack on Data | |
|---|---|---|---|---|
| | **Disable** | **Overprovide** | **Manipulate** | **Steal** |
| Engine control | Halts | Fuel inefficiency; unpredictable motion | N/A | N/A |
| Propulsion control | Slowing; slowness | Speeding; acceleration | N/A | N/A |
| Brake control | Does not slow down or halt | Slows down or halts when not needed | N/A | N/A |
| Steering control | Drifts out of path; fails to avoid obstacle | Spins out of path; fails to avoid obstacle | N/A | N/A |
| Power control | Control units stop functioning | Control units may be damaged by power surge | N/A | N/A |
| Safety control (air bags, etc.) | Air bags do not deploy when needed | Air bags deploy when not needed | N/A | N/A |
| Stability control | Drifts out of path | Spins out of path | N/A | N/A |
| Body control (door locks, windows, etc.) | Endangers safety | Denies access | N/A | N/A |
| Navigation | Gets lost | Gets lost | May reach a different destination | Privacy loss caused by stolen travel patterns |
| LiDAR/camera | Blinding | Blinding | Spoofing | N/A |
| V2V communication | Cannot communicate with other vehicles | Confounds other vehicles through overcommunication | Confounds other vehicles through miscommunication | N/A |

**Table 3.1—continued**

| Function/ Control Unit | Hack on Component | | Hack on Data | |
|---|---|---|---|---|
| | Disable | Overprovide | Manipulate | Steal |
| V2I communication | Cannot communicate with transport infrastructure | Confounds the infrastructure through overcom-munication | Confounds the infrastructure through miscom-munication | N/A |
| Over-the-air update | Continues to use outdated or vulnerable software | Hampers normal operation due to repeated updates | Installs malware | N/A |
| Onboard diagnostics | Displays no diagnostic information | Displays unnecessary diagnostic information | Displays incorrect diagnostic information | Privacy loss |

CHAPTER FOUR

# Hacked Autonomous Vehicles and the Harms They Can Cause

The previous chapter focused on the hacking risks to AV systems. To enable our later analysis of liability, this chapter explores the damage that a hacked vehicle might cause. To date, there have not been many publicly reported incidents involving damages caused by a hacked AV.[1] Therefore, this chapter opens with a discussion of various categories of scenarios that might allow a hacked AV to inflict real-world harms.

The scenarios we developed possess several attributes:

- They are based on real-world events.
- They describe multiple types of hackers.
- They describe exploitation of vulnerabilities in different AV systems.
- They describe a wide range of real-world consequences.

First, we note several important observations about how hacked AVs will change the risks vis-à-vis the current driving environment. Threats involving vehicles with a human driver generally require attackers to be physically close to their targets, while hackers may be able to attack AVs remotely. Vulnerabilities in conventional vehicles' mechanical systems are relatively few, easy to mitigate, and difficult to

---

[1] There have been crashes caused by system programming, tracking devices have been planted on cars, and a Federal Bureau of Investigation–National Highway Traffic Safety Administration (NHTSA) warning about vehicle hacking being on the rise was issued, but a car has not been driven off the road outside a controlled test environment.

exploit en masse. AV vulnerabilities are complex, numerous, and likely to be widespread. The consequences of those threats acting on those vulnerabilities set the stage for our liability analysis.

In terms of consequences, computer hacking of AVs implicates fast, heavy, potentially dangerous objects. Successful commandeering of an AV provides an attacker with a 4,000-pound projectile that they may be able to route as they please to achieve mayhem. An AV that can accelerate from 0 to 60 miles per hour (mph) in under 3 seconds can create a force of nearly 23 kilonewtons (kN). The same AV traveling at 100 mph represents nearly 2.5 megajoules (MJ) of kinetic energy. Larger payloads, such as a truck or tractor-trailer, can increase that number by an order of magnitude. We explore aspects of the destructive potential of these wheeled, computerized, autonomous projectiles in Chapter Seven's scenarios.

The remainder of this chapter is divided into five sections.

- The first section briefly discusses the set of real-world events that we reviewed.
- The second introduces the types of attackers that AVs will likely contend with.
- The third discusses the types of vulnerabilities we considered.
- The fourth enumerates the types of real-world consequences we identified.
- The fifth offers conclusions and identifies an additional step required for civil liability analysis of our scenario fact patterns that is covered in the next chapter.

## Examples of Vehicles Causing Damage

We sought to use real-world events as a starting point for our scenarios to maintain plausibility and demonstrate that these scenarios are foreseeable. Given the early-stage development of AV technology, examples of hacked AVs in the wild are difficult to come by, but there is no shortage of news about how regular vehicles, or AVs that were not hacked, cause damage every day. Two main strains draw attention:

Vehicles with human drivers accidentally crash into things all the time. Also, intentional acts cause real-world damages: Witness several recent examples of terrorists using vehicles in ramming attacks. By analyzing the real-world examples of each type of event, our scenarios can better anticipate what might happen if hacks on AVs succeed. The remainder of this section explores examples of both AVs and human drivers causing damage in the real world.

### Damage from Autonomous Vehicles Without Hacking

Several high-profile incidents involving Alphabet Inc.'s Google (now Waymo), Uber Technologies Inc., and Tesla Inc. have revealed some of the dangers involved with AVs already on the road. These examples lack both an attacker and a nexus to cybersecurity. But they demonstrate the consequences of AV system failure.

One of Google's first reported AV incidents involved a car attempting to turn into a lane occupied by an oncoming bus (Associated Press, 2016). The software incorrectly assumed that the bus driver would let the car into the lane, and a collision occurred. In a similar incident, a self-driving Uber vehicle was reported to have run a red light (Levin, 2016). Fortunately, there were no casualties and only minor damage to the car in the first event and no damages at all in the second event. In the Tesla example, however, the vehicle's autopilot system failed to detect a major obstacle on the highway, and the person in the driver's seat died in the resulting crash (Yadron and Tynan, 2016). More recently, an Uber vehicle hit and killed a pedestrian who was pushing a bicycle with plastic bags on it (Marshall and Davies, 2018).

From these examples, we can conclude that there are already instances of AVs failing in ways that cause harm. That harm can result from the design and logic of the system, as in the Google example, or it can result from failures of a system's ability to correctly sense the environment, as in the Uber and Tesla examples.

### Unintentional Damage from Vehicles with Human Drivers

Examples from this category lack an attacker, a connection to AV-specific systems, or a nexus to cybersecurity. They are nevertheless the most prevalent damage scenario, so there are a vast number of incidents to choose from. These include damage to critical infrastructure, such as bridges (Gutierrez and Helsel, 2016) and overpasses (Bulwa and Fimrite, 2007), and compromise of sensitive cargo, ranging from toxic chemicals (Shipeng, 2008) to missiles falling out of military convoys on highways ("Truck with Missiles Crashes in Louisiana," 1993). It may seem obvious, but part of what these examples show is that vehicles are everywhere and the potential for damage is significant—even when there is no adversary trying to cause harm.

One real-world example illustrates the range of physical targets that have yet to be hardened against vehicles that hackers may transform into projectiles. A story that began with a highway pursuit of an SUV ended with $60 million of damages to a U.S. Navy fighter plane when the SUV crashed through an air base's perimeter defenses and collided with the parked aircraft (Lendon, 2016). This example shows the potential scale of a single incident and raises the question of which party bears the responsibility to defend vulnerable targets—and restricted areas—from rogue vehicles.

We extracted several observations from these examples:

- Vehicles are in close proximity to a wide variety of targets, making the potential real-world damages exceptionally broad.
- The scale of even a single incident can be huge (Wiedeman, 2016; Pagliery, 2015).
- The burden to defend sites against weaponized vehicles is shared and ambiguous.

### Intentional Damage from Vehicles with Human Drivers

This category of attacks illustrates how attackers currently employ vehicles in a range of crimes. These examples do not include hacks, but as those opportunities emerge, liability analysis will be needed.

"Crash and grab" crimes occupy the lower end of this spectrum. Much like its "smash and grab" predecessor, which involved such tactics as breaking car windows to steal Christmas presents, this variant uses vehicles to breach larger barriers, such as the entrance to a building. That access enables the theft of high-value targets, such as an

ATM from a convenience store or jewelry from a jeweler (O'Connell, Thayer, and Panzar, 2015; Reiter, 2014).

Cargo theft is another example of a common and extremely costly type of theft (Grushkin, 2011; Stock, Wagner, and Escamilla, 2012). Hijacking tractor-trailers or just making off with their cargo while they are at a rest stop are both examples that could easily be mimicked by AV hackers.

More-tragic examples than theft must be considered here too. Recent terrorist attacks in New York, Spain (Bolon, Karasz, and McKinley, Jr., 2017), Nice (Herridge and Tomlinson, 2016), and Berlin[2] involved an attacker gaining control of a large vehicle and driving it at high speed through areas crowded with pedestrians.

These examples again raise a question that bears on the liability framework that we will examine later in this analysis: Who has the burden to defend against attacks when vehicles become weaponized by a terrorist at the wheel or a cyberattacker at the keyboard? These examples demonstrate the following:

- Criminals already use vehicles to cause real-world harm.
- Attackers will seek to maximize the damage they cause.
- Responsibility for defending targets against these threats is unclear.

## Potential Hackers and Their Motivations

How might different types of attackers use hacked AVs to achieve their goals? For the purpose of this analysis, it is sufficient to say that the motivations and capabilities of different types of bad actors determine the scope and nature of their actions (Ganor, 2005). A model that describes levels of mischief sought by cyberattackers (the left column in Table 4.1) provides a starting point for thinking about types of actors

---

[2] It is worth noting as a counterpoint that, in the second attack in Berlin, reports suggested that automated braking systems on the truck prevented even greater damage (Dearden, 2016). However, if an attacker has compromised the vehicle's steering and acceleration, they may also be able to disable the automated braking.

**Table 4.1**
**Typical Characteristics of Cyber Threats**

| Level | Typical Actors | Typical Motivations and Capabilities of Typical Actors |
|---|---|---|
| 1<br>Cyber vandalism | Hackers, taggers, "script kiddies" (who use code written by others), and small disaffected groups of the above | Disrupt or embarrass the victimized organization (e.g., a specific department or federal government as a whole) |
| 2<br>Cyber theft/ crime | Individuals or small, loosely affiliated groups; political or ideological activists; terrorists; domestic insiders; industrial spies; spammers | Obtain critical information and/or usurp or disrupt the organization's business or mission functions for profit or ideological use |
| 3<br>Cyber incursion/ surveillance | Nation-state government entity; patriotic hacker group; sophisticated terrorist group; professional organized criminal enterprise | Increase knowledge of general infrastructure; plant seeds for future attacks. Obtain or modify specific information and/or disrupt cyber resources, specifically resources associated with missions or even information types |
| 4<br>Cyber sabotage/ espionage | Professional intelligence organization or military service operative | Obtain specific, high-value information; undermine or impede critical aspects of a mission, program, or enterprise; or place itself in a position to do so in the future |
| 5<br>Cyber conflict/ warfare | Nation-state military possibly supported by their intelligence service; very sophisticated and capable insurgent or terrorist group | Severely undermine or destroy an organization's use of its mission, information, and/or infrastructure |

(middle column) and their motivations and capabilities (right column) (Bodeau, Graubart, and Fabius, 2010).

Because our focus is on conventional civil liability risks, we focus our analysis on levels 1–3 (individual hackers of various capabilities, small groups of them, activists, industrial spies, sophisticated terrorist hackers or nation states, and organized crime) and leave out the most sophisticated actors in levels 4 and 5. Although those actors (intelligence organizations, military operatives, nation states, or very sophisticated terrorist groups) may possess the most powerful capabilities, the consequences of their actions may not be covered by civil liability. For example, if a nation state attacked another by compromising every AV on the road at the same time, the consequences would be enormous, but it might be considered an act of war and thus would typically be excluded under insurance policies, at least if attribution of the attack to a nation state was clear.[3] Victims might seek redress against the entity responsible for the attack, but this would be challenging. Further exploration of the civil liability implications of large-scale attacks or those conducted by nation states would be very useful but are outside the scope of this report.

We augment Table 4.1, which already addresses intents as "typical motivations," with examples that suggest the capabilities that might be put into use in the context of AVs (Table 4.2).

It is, nevertheless, worth pointing out that capabilities move fluidly in the cyber domain—once vulnerabilities are known, attacks can become weaponized and disseminated extremely quickly across the various levels of actors enumerated in Table 4.1 ("Dark Motives Online: An Analysis of Overlapping Technologies Used by Cybercriminals and Terrorist Organizations," 2016). For example, researchers at Tencent, a major internet company based in China, recently discovered vulnerabilities in Tesla vehicles that, once exploited, led to a compromise so

**Table 4.2**
**Autonomous Vehicle Hackers' Intentions**

| Level | Motivation | Capability | Use |
|---|---|---|---|
| 1<br>Cyber vandalism | Disruption or embarrassment | Reuse others' attacks on unpatched systems | Change highway sign |
| 2<br>Cyber theft or crime | Disruption for profit or ideology | Hack OBD-II port on parked car or connected systems | Trigger ransomware |
| 3<br>Cyber incursion/ surveillance | Breach or disruption of mission systems | Hack back-end systems | Infiltrate fleet's or manufacturer's connected systems |

[3] See, generally, Doherty, 2017.

complete that a vehicle's brakes could be disabled remotely while the vehicle was moving. These researchers published their discovery online and included a YouTube video demonstration (Keen Security Lab of Tencent, 2016).

Given this description of the types of hackers who may attack AVs, what kinds of attacks might each level launch? The following sections illustrate the types of attacks that may correspond to each of the first three levels.

### Level 1—Cyber Vandalism

The actors in this category will be at the low ends of both the skill and motivation spectrums. They are less likely to discover new zero-day flaws or to develop new exploits of those flaws, but they will be capable of targeting unpatched systems with exploits created by others. Most well-defended systems will be able to resist this type of attacker, but many systems without significant defenses will be vulnerable.

One example of this type of attacker might be an angry neighbor. In the same way that physical proximity has led to neighbors hacking into Wi-Fi routers, AVs could also become targets. In some cases, the damages from this type of threat actor will be a minor nuisance, but in others they can be much more serious (Kravets, 2011). For example, a hack that disables an ignition circuit may strand a driver in their driveway and make the target late for work. That same hack executed while the car is traveling in the fast lane could be life-threatening.

### Level 2—Cyber Theft or Crime

This category of attacker will possess at least a moderate level of skill and, more importantly, a relatively high degree of motivation, primarily financial. They may be able to discover new zero-day vulnerabilities. Even if they cannot, they will aggressively seek to use vulnerabilities and exploits discovered by others and will not hesitate to apply sophisticated tools, such as crimeware kits and services (Weise, 2016).

Given the profit motive, attackers in this category might turn to ransomware. Cars are often the second–most expensive asset an individual owns (after a home), so if an attacker can hold a car hostage, they might be able to secure a moderate ransom to release it.

Notably, this category also includes insider attacks. An insider in the context of AVs might be the owners themselves seeking to cover their tracks while using the vehicle to cause harm and subsequently blaming the system or manufacturer. AV event recorders will mitigate this to some extent, but not entirely (Musk, 2013). Of greater concern are both the privacy and physical security risks associated with insiders operating AVs' back-end systems. When such insider actors decide to attack, they will, by definition, have much better access to back-end systems than the cyber vandals described in level 1 in Table 4.1 (Evans, 2016).

### Level 3—Cyber Incursion or Surveillance

The more sophisticated actors in this category will likely be able to breach AV systems without help from other parties. They will therefore have the potential to cause severe harm. Furthermore, their objectives might not be financial. Although insurance policies may exclude coverage for acts of war and terrorism, public attribution (identifying culprits) for cyberattacks continues to be a challenge (Goodin, 2016). It is an open question whether claims can be rejected based on the scale of an attack alone—that is, without conclusively attributing a large-scale attack to a state actor or terrorist group. If those claims cannot be rejected, civil liability may come into play.

Among hacker groups that are aligned with a particular government, professional organized crime syndicates, and sophisticated terrorist groups, it is the terrorists who are most likely to claim responsibility for an attack as part of their modus operandi, even perhaps for attacks that they did not cause. Others will be more circumspect, leaving greater ambiguity when it comes to attribution. What we do know, however, is that terrorists are willing to kill, they are specifically thinking about using AVs for more-devastating vehicle attacks (Pleskot, 2016; Atherton, 2016), and they are actively inciting "lone wolves" to action. Traditional barriers to litigation may not hold forever against victims seeking remedies from terrorist events (Marmouyet, 2016; Steinhauer, Mazzetti, and Hirschfeld Davis, 2016; Fiegerman, 2016; Williams, 2016).

This examination of the threat landscape provides greater clarity about the motivations and capabilities of potential attackers.[4] We now turn to a brief review of the types of targets that may be vulnerable.

## Targets That Are Vulnerable to Hacked Autonomous Vehicles

Conventional vehicles are ubiquitous and can go nearly anywhere. That is unlikely to change with AVs. An attacker with remote control of an AV will be able to choose from a wide variety of targets while potentially remaining anonymous. If that is the case, and if additional defensive measures are not put in place, many new types of targets will be vulnerable merely because of reduced deterrence—specifically, bad actors will have less chance of getting caught, injured, or killed (Federal Aviation Administration, 2016).

Mitigations can protect some targets from the risk of AVs used as projectiles. Bollards and other barriers protect military and government buildings or other structures with high security requirements. Similarly, geofencing built into AV navigation systems that prohibits entry into particular places may also provide a layer of protection.

While it is difficult to quantify the danger that AVs pose, it is also difficult to deny the fundamental changes they bring to risks to existing buildings, structures, and other environments. Taking the example of "crash and grab" crime, if AVs make this easier to do, there will be some cost to businesses to protect themselves from the threat—through either insurance or guards and physical barriers.

Several types of real-world harms result from car accidents or intentional acts:

- human casualties (Rubin, Briscoe, and Landsberg, 2003)

---

[4] An alternative to thinking about how computer experts would use AVs and infrastructure to produce cyber effects is thinking about how those with physical orientations and objectives might employ AVs and infrastructure to those ends. This latter analysis is beyond the scope of our current effort.

- property damage—including compromising sensitive cargo (Li, 2010)
- economic losses ("Ram-Raid Gang Steals Cash Machine," 2007)
- damage to the environment (Sumra et al., 2011)
- damage to critical infrastructure (Sturgeon, 2016; Wright, 2011; Montgomery, 2015).

For categories of vulnerable targets like critical infrastructure and the environment, secondary effects might also cause significant harm. For example, taking out a power substation with a car can cause harms such as business interruption and loss of revenue. Likewise, polluting a body of water by driving a tanker truck full of toxic materials into it can, in addition to causing health or environmental problems, reduce nearby property values. Liability for these secondary damages may need to be accounted for when managing the risk of hacked AVs.

The fact that in these examples such targets are vulnerable to attack from a single vehicle highlights how powerful commandeered vehicles can be as weapons. In addition to the short and general list above, caution also suggests reevaluating categories of critical infrastructure risk as the U.S. Department of Homeland Security has defined them.

Presidential Policy Directive 21, "Critical Infrastructure Security and Resilience," identifies 16 sectors of critical infrastructure (U.S. Department of Homeland Security, 2016):

- chemical
- commercial facilities
- communications
- critical manufacturing
- dams
- defense industrial base
- emergency services
- energy
- financial services
- food and agriculture
- government facilities

- health care and public health
- information technology
- nuclear reactors, materials, and waste
- transportation systems
- water and wastewater systems.

For many of these sectors, it may be difficult to imagine an attacker from levels 1–3 of our framework who could both successfully target them and produce consequences that fall in the scope of civil liability. However, some sectors do seem more likely targets than others.

The commercial facilities sector is perhaps the most relevant inventory of relatively vulnerable targets. The description identifies the following attributes of sites in this category (U.S. Department of Homeland Security, 2017):

- They comprise a diverse range of sites.
- They draw large crowds.
- They operate on the principle of open public access.
- The majority are privately owned and operated.

Even outside the context of analyzing civil liability, facilities that fall within the eight subsectors of this sector (as listed in Table 4.3) might need to revisit their defensive postures if and when hackers weaponize AVs. In terms of liability analysis, the foreseeability of damages from such attacks will break new legal ground.

Having identified many categories of existing targets that will become more vulnerable to attacks from hacked AVs, in the next section, we turn to analyzing the types of damage that attackers inflict on those targets. With that analysis in hand, we will proceed to a legal analysis of civil liability.

**Table 4.3**
**Commercial Facilities Subsectors**

| Subsector | Example Facility |
|---|---|
| Entertainment and media | motion picture studios, broadcast media |
| Gaming | casinos |
| Lodging | hotels, motels, conference centers |
| Outdoor events | theme and amusement parks, fairs, campgrounds, parades |
| Public assembly | arenas, stadiums, aquariums, zoos, museums, convention centers |
| Real estate | office and apartment buildings, condominiums, mixed-use facilities, self-storage |
| Retail | retail centers and districts, shopping malls |
| Sports leagues | professional sports leagues and federations |

## What Types of Harm Can Hacked Autonomous Vehicles Cause?

The types of damages that result from attackers using AVs flow directly out of the vulnerabilities identified in the previous section. Human targets will result in casualties, fatalities, psychological distress, and loss of privacy. Property damage will include harm to buildings, valuable goods, land, the AVs themselves, and other vehicles. Pure economic losses (such as lost business) are also possible (Du, 2015; Rojas, 2015; Connecticut Department of Transportation, undated; Root, 2016). These cases have traditionally been more difficult for plaintiffs to make (Galligan et al., 2007), particularly those involving hacking.

For reasons we explain in a subsequent chapter, it might be easier for plaintiffs to recover damages resulting from hacked AVs than from data breaches (Smith, 2013). In the case of a data breach, even when plaintiffs have had their identities stolen, the courts have challenged the plaintiffs to show that the identity theft was connected to the data breach because the same data could have been stolen from many other places. These challenges may be easier to overcome when a hacked vehicle leaves a trail of wreckage.

Damage to the environment and damage to critical infrastructure both raise the issue of second-order effects. If hazardous materials are released into a body of water or a city, the consequences include not only the direct cleanup and mitigation costs but also the potential loss in value to the surrounding property. Similarly, complex attacks (Loukas, undated) might use a hacked AV to turn off the electricity, if even only in a small area, to enable subsequent stages of a more elaborate attack.

## Conclusions

In this chapter, we have discussed the real-world events we used to ground our later liability analysis scenarios, and we have considered the harms that can result from successful hacking of AVs.

The model we used to identify potential harms suggests that the most dangerous actors (states and terrorists) may not be the most relevant to an analysis of civil liability. However, there are still several very capable actors that are within the scope of civil liability that also have motives that would lead to damages. And we should not underestimate the sophistication of the cyber threat facing AV systems, given hackers' ability to reuse previously discovered attacks, the availability of entire architectures that can be provisioned to support malware attacks, and the general challenges that have vexed computer network defenders for decades.

Due to the vast road system in the United States, AVs are likely to have access to vulnerable targets of every description. Many of these targets will become more vulnerable because AVs can be deployed remotely, eliminating the need for drivers willing to put themselves at risk. Those vulnerabilities will be balanced against defenses to prevent hacked AVs. At the AV system level, significant defenses will be in place: It will not be easy to hack an AV. However, given our cybersecurity track record in other areas, it would be naïve to assume that these defense systems will always succeed. Thus, the scenarios and liability analysis in this report are needed. Caution suggests at least considering the real-world vulnerabilities that AVs will introduce or increase, identifying who may bear the responsibility to mitigate threats or pay damages, and understanding the way that those potential damages may create incentives to minimize the risk of hacking or mitigate the damages that it can cause.

CHAPTER FIVE

# Shifting Roles and Responsibilities for Information Assurance for Autonomous Vehicle Cybersecurity

This chapter examines the roles and responsibilities of parties who may face liability for damages from hacked AVs. It also considers how their roles might change as new models of ownership and AV use evolve. For example, while vehicle owners today share in the duties of maintenance, those roles might change when it comes to assuring the cybersecurity of an AV in the era of over-the-air software updates and on-demand ride sharing. Given the prospective nature of this analysis, it does not endeavor to predict the future. Rather, it selectively analyzes aspects of potential futures to consider how relationships between stakeholders in the AV economy may change.

This analysis discusses which parties may have primary responsibility for cyber assurance of AVs across various phases of the cars' production and service lives. Then it will explore how those parties' roles in information assurance—the protection of relevant data—may shift and be shared in new ways. The possible shifts in responsibility will be analyzed using a framework that connects various stakeholders to the four stages of an AV's development and use: design and manufacture, sale or lease, service life, and the provision of market protections (such as regulations, insurance, warranties, and other mechanisms) throughout its life cycle. In conclusion, the chapter will highlight key issues for policymakers to consider based on how roles will change and how responsibilities will be shared in a future of AVs.

Overall, we can anticipate greater need to assure the integrity of the information that AVs collect, use, or produce to ensure AV cybersecurity. For example, hackers might be interested in exploiting data about a driver's route or surroundings that could be collected by its GPS system and onboard cameras. The parties who may play roles in AV information assurance include car owners (corporate or individual), riders in cars operated by companies offering transportation services (e.g., a rideshare passenger), manufacturers, dealers, or others. Currently, it is not clear how well protection of vehicle data is being managed. The future is even less certain in this regard.

In the future, information assurance will likely be addressed not only through manufacturing and point of sale but also through maintenance, failure detection, and repairs. It will likely also be shared among parties. With regard to maintenance, private owners may have responsibility for accepting over-the-air updates that maintain cybersecurity of various components. That maintenance responsibility may be shared with manufacturers who can monitor completion of updates. Roles in detecting cyber vulnerabilities may also be shared. For example, manufacturers made aware of defects would surely be responsible for issuing patches, while owners and users of AVs could be obligated to take action when they become aware of vulnerabilities. A need to repair or update components that affect cybersecurity may fall to multiple parties, with owners being responsible for taking a car to a shop or dealership for repairs or manufacturers being responsible for disabling cars with vulnerabilities to prevent damages from malicious hackers. The allocation of legal responsibilities arising from these roles will be a matter for courts and policymakers to take up as the technology proliferates. As these examples illustrate, proliferation of AVs could bring wide distribution responsibility for information assurance.

## Parties Responsible for Automotive Cybersecurity

Any discussion of liability requires identification of the parties involved and a determination of who takes charge of which responsibilities over time. This discussion of these responsibilities for AV cybersecurity employs two frameworks. The first framework comes from NIST, which provides a list of stakeholders. Our second framework outlines the likely phases of vehicle development. (See Appendix B for a consolidated table of the phases of vehicle development.) Here, we analyze the roles of selected stakeholders and potential changes in the roles through each phase.

### Identifying Stakeholders in the NIST Cyber-Physical Systems Framework

This analysis of stakeholder roles in cyber assurance makes use of the NIST Cyber-Physical Systems Framework (National Institute of Standards and Technology and CPS Public Working Group, 2017). The framework is intended to aid in understanding the relationships and responsibilities involved in the internet of things—connected devices like AVs that have both cyber and physical elements. This framework can help structure the analyses of how relationships between relevant players may change as AVs become more common.

This analysis modifies and expands the current NIST CPS draft guidance where needed vis-à-vis AVs. Current guidance in the NIST CPS framework names ten stakeholder classes for the development of products in many domains or industries. Our analysis expands this framework to 12 stakeholder classes and adapts it to the automotive setting, adding dealerships/aftermarket installers and the public as follows:

1. creators/manufacturers (of cars, hardware, and software, including infrastructure as service and hyperscale cloud providers—e.g., Amazon Web Services, Microsoft Azure)
2. supply chain providers (of components or intellectual property)
3. service providers (e.g., consultants, contractors, bankers, repair shops, lawyers)
4. competitors (in the development, market offering, and service life phases)
5. dealers/aftermarket installers (of cars and parts)
6. customers (e.g., car purchasers/payers and users)
7. owners (either individuals or corporations)

8. operators (either individuals or corporations)
9. insurers
10. regulators
11. government
12. the public.

## Comparing Responsibilities in the Phases of Vehicle Development and Use

These stakeholders' roles and responsibilities in an AV future will be analyzed through four phases of a vehicle's life cycle, using a framework adapted for this analysis from the NHTSA (NHTSA, 2016a; Rana et al., 2014):

- Phase 1: Production and development (design, engineering,
- manufacturing)
- Phase 2: Market offering (sale or lease)
- Phase 3: Transportation service life (use by owner or rider)
- Phase 4: Market protections (regulations, insurance, warranties).

In Figures 5.1 and 5.2, these four phases are depicted first in the context of the current state of the industry and then in the future state, when AVs become more widespread.

Figure 5.1 shows the linear progression of Phase 1 (production), Phase 2 (sale/lease), and Phase 3 (service life). Phase 4 (market protection through insurance or regulations) spans the lifetime of the vehicle.

**Figure 5.1**
**Current Phases of Vehicle Development and Use**

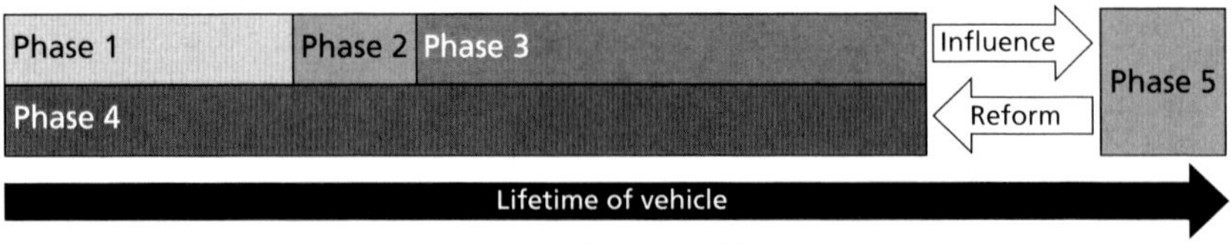


Phase 1 — Production and development (design and manufacturing)
Phase 2 — Market offering (sale or lease)
Phase 3 — Transportation service life (use and maintenance)
Phase 4 — Market protections (insurance, regulations)
Phase 5 — Societal response (reaction of public to each phase)

**Figure 5.2**
**Emerging Phases of Vehicle Development and Use**

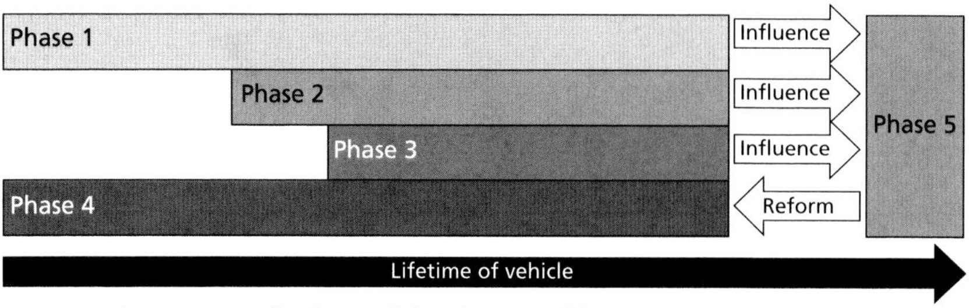


Phase 1 — Production and development (design and manufacturing)
Phase 2 — Market offering (sale or lease)
Phase 3 — Transportation service life (use and maintenance)
Phase 4 — Market protections (insurance, regulations)
Phase 5 — Societal response (reaction of public to each phase)

In Phase 5, which we do not cover in this report, society reacts to stakeholder actions in Phases 1–3 and provides feedback that may motivate consumer protections in Phase 4.

Figure 5.2 shows the expansion of roles and responsibilities that may occur in a future substantially affected by AVs. Phase 1 (production) may persist for the life of the vehicle, as manufacturers must build and update information assurance features. Phase 2 (sale or lease) may also persist from sale point until end of vehicle life if sellers or lessors take part in maintenance of information assurance features. Phase 3 (service life) is unchanged from the model depicted in Figure 5.1. Phase 4 (market protection through insurance or regulations) still spans the lifetime of the vehicle. In this conception of phases of AV use, Phase 5 is informed by all other phases as society adjusts to stakeholders' reactions and provides feedback that may reform regulations in Phase 4.

## Comparing Responsibilities in Phases of Vehicle Development and Use

As the figures show, market protections, such as regulations, warranties, or insurance coverage (Phase 4), span all phases of the vehicle life cycle, both now and in the future. Expected changes in the future are shown with the expansion of production and development (Phase 1) and market offering (Phase 2) to persist until the end of a vehicle's service life. Phase 1 is longer in the future because vehicle design may be changed (e.g., through software updates that raise or lower ride height or other factors) after the point of sale or lease. Already, elements of Phase 2, that of market offering in the form of sale, lease, or rental, are changing because of car-sharing business models.

Our analysis also takes into account societal response (including legal response) to changes in each of these phases and how that might ripple back through the AV economy to affect market protections, such as insurance coverage or regulations.

## Phase-by-Phase Analysis of Shifts in Roles and Responsibilities

In this section, we analyze each phase to highlight potential shifts among the relationships between stakeholders for information assurance of AVs as the market evolves.

### Phase 1: Development and Production

The NIST development and production phase includes several stakeholders:

- creators/manufacturers
- supply chain providers
- service providers, such as consultants and contractors.

Currently, the development and production phase of new vehicle models takes years. This process allows designers to take into account motor vehicle codes and regulations.[1]

---

1 For an overview of the requirements for manufacturers of motor vehicles and motor vehicle equipment, see NHTSA (2016b).

### *Creators and Manufacturers*

In the future, creators and manufacturers will likely have to recalibrate design, manufacturing, and testing to ensure safety and cybersecurity as AV functions are updated using over-the-air updates (Porges, 2015). The potential for software updates to be offered or sold for multiple years after release of the vehicle model speaks to these shifts in responsibility. The trend toward the ability of users to access any data, in any location, using any device likely will drive manufacturers to further consider security up front in the product life cycle, as well as later. This is implicated by the overlap of Phase 1 with Phases 2 and 3 in Figure 5.2. Should manufacturers and suppliers offer post-delivery vehicle improvements, they need to protect both the vehicle and the manufacturing/design facilities from cyberattack.

### *Supply Chain Providers*

Supply chain providers, such as component manufacturers, will also have to adjust practices to meet information assurance needs for AVs. They may have to enhance their hardware components and any complementary software to provide assurance for machine-to-machine communications. Automated communication in AVs allows for consistency in vehicle functionality. For example, in the case of automated brake control, a series of steps takes place between identification of a threat by the forward collision warning system and the brake actuator control. At each step, communication takes place. Supply chain providers also will need to protect communications access across components of the CAN bus and other in-vehicle communication networks. Information assurance will likely require components designed to use authentication keys and certificates for approval to receive or issue commands.

To avoid introducing vulnerabilities, parties that supply aftermarket features or develop software for vehicles on the road will have to adjust to vehicle changes or updates initiated by suppliers and manufacturers. For example, continuous updates in features to improve an AV's competitiveness on the market (e.g., network-enabled services and entertainment) will carry a recurring cost of security testing and validation for the vehicle platform and the newly integrated feature.

### *Service Providers*

Based on their experiences with AVs themselves and any user testing or focus groups they conduct, consultants and contractors should provide insight and awareness relevant to AV information assurance to automotive manufacturers and supply chain providers. See Table 5.1.

## Phase 2: Market Offering

Our adaptation of the NIST CPS framework implicates the following stakeholders in the market offering phase:

- dealers and aftermarket installers of parts or services
- customers and users of vehicles
- service providers, such as financial institutions.

The market offering stage may change stakeholder roles and responsibilities in multiple ways as concepts like car sharing change practices around vehicle ownership. The current distribution system for conventional vehicles uses a broad network of distribution for sale or leasing via dealerships, as well as a used-vehicle market. Aftermarket products allow for modification or replacement of such features as stereos, wheels, and suspension parts.

**Table 5.1**
**Expansion of Responsibility in the Development and Production Phase**

| Stakeholder Roles | Potential Expansion in Responsibility vis-à-vis Information Assurance |
|---|---|
| Creators and manufacturers | • Ongoing feature development for released models to maintain competitiveness<br>• Machine-to-machine communication security<br>• Protection of authentication keys and certificates |
| Supply chain providers | • Machine-to-machine communication security<br>• Protection of authentication keys and certificates for features beyond driving (e.g., entertainment systems) |
| Service providers (contractors/consultants) | • Machine-to-machine communication security<br>• Protection of authentication keys and certificates for features beyond driving |

While it is difficult to project exactly how ownership patterns will change in a future of AVs, for the purposes of this discussion, we will examine scenarios in which some people still own cars individually while others use a variety of on-demand driving services. Thus, ownership of vehicles is expected to partially shift away from individuals to corporate entities that offer rides. This indicates that market offering of vehicles, at least in the context of on-demand ride services, will increasingly involve repeat transactions for vehicle use under a primary owner.

In order to better understand the potential shifts in roles during market offering, we can examine ownership and operation. Table 5.2 illustrates some models of vehicle market offering in the context of on-demand car and ride services. In these current models, custody of a vehicle can be authorized for a separate operator over the course of hours, days, weeks, and months. Expectations about roles and responsibilities between stakeholders change when AV users find vehicles to use temporarily via a mobile app and then retrieve them across dispersed lots, dedicated parking spots, and personal driveways.

We can look at how responsibility is shared for auto insurance, refueling, and general maintenance in these ride-for-hire models to understand how cyber protection responsibilities may be shared. In car-sharing services, payment for refueling and the physical act of

**Table 5.2**
**On-Demand Car Service Models and Examples**

| | Examples | |
|---|---|---|
| **Ownership Model** | **User Drives Vehicle** | **User Rides in Vehicle (Chauffeured or AV)** |
| Manufacturer owns car | • Car2Go (Mercedes-Benz)<br>• GoDrive (Ford) | • Maven (General Motors [GM])<br>• Kango (Fiat Chrysler) |
| Third party owns car | • ZipCar (Avis Rent-a-Car) | • Taxi<br>• Lyft<br>• Uber<br>• Waymo |
| Individual owner | • Turo | • Jitney drivers<br>• Executive car services |

filling the tank have been shared between owner and operator. For example, ZipCar asks users to refuel using its purchase card, while traditional car rental companies will fill the tank for a fee. General maintenance in all these cases fall on the owner of the vehicle. The diversity of emerging models will present challenges to dealers, buyers, and financers as AVs appear on the market. However, fleet ownership may provide benefits in terms of systematic fleet maintenance and routine installation of updates.

With regard to information assurance, imagine a scenario in which rideshare customers go to the same parking lot each day and select an AV that will drive them home after work. That habit may create new types of cyber vulnerabilities vis-à-vis hackers who try to exploit such routines with targeted attacks. Stakeholders will need to protect customer identities that could be targeted by hackers in those scenarios. Those stronger protections could take the form of manufacturers, dealerships, or car-sharing company owners adding information assurance protections to AVs. They could also require protection of the data servers that support smart infrastructure, such as parking lots, car distribution algorithms, and sharing applications.

#### *Car Dealers and Rental Companies*

Many factors indicate that individual ownership of vehicles will persist in the future. Vehicle dealerships will need to evolve with cybersecurity in mind because their role in maintenance may continue to extend through the life of the vehicle. The same caution applies to rental companies. From the standpoint of both buyers and users, responsibilities for information assurance must be clarified upon transfer of vehicles and in ongoing communications or messages delivered to owners or users via the AV.

Dealers and businesses that rent cars or offer rides may need to react to information assurance challenges in many other ways:

- They may need to monitor AV or smart transportation system messages to ensure that malware is not transmitted.
- Just as Transportation Safety Administration announcements in the airport caution travelers not to accept any packages from

people they do not know, AVs may use similar messaging for downloads that AV users attempt to make from untrusted sources.

- During transfer or resale, the practices akin to those currently employed for cleaning the cabin interior will likely have to extend to the car's electronics and memory. In other words, a digital scrubbing will be required.
- Sales of vehicles to companies that provide rideshare services may call for third parties who specialize in offering security products (i.e., data monitoring and insurance coverage) to customers and owners, as well as end users. Likewise, customers or end users may wish to adopt security monitoring services and insurance coverages. See Table 5.3.

As noted, the deployment of AVs on a large scale likely implies that the roles and responsibilities of stakeholders in the market offering phase will change to ensure information assurance. In the context of AV dealerships, everything from staffing to maintenance procedures to both pre- and post-sale communication with buyers about information assurance are subject to changes. In the context of AV rentals, the future will likely require similar evolutions in communication between company and customer, as well as clear delineations of responsibility for information assurance maintenance.

### Phase 3: Transportation Service Life

In the transportation service life phase, roles and responsibilities for information assurance, and potential liability flowing from those roles, will also become more complex and likely will shift. Under the current

**Table 5.3**
**Expansion of Responsibilities in the Market Offering Phase**

| Stakeholder Role | Potential Expansion in Responsibility vis-à-vis Information Assurance |
|---|---|
| Dealers and rental agencies | • Protection of AV delivery channels and user identity and location |
| Customers and users | • Comprehension of information-sharing agreements<br>• Consideration of identity monitoring and financial protection services |

system for conventional vehicles, those roles have developed organically and by regulation and are well defined. The stakeholders relevant to this phase in the NIST CPS framework are

- owners
- operators
- customers/users
- service providers (including repair shops).

***Owners, Operators, and Customers/Users***

The future relationships among owners, operators, and customers/users of AVs are likely to change, with each of those actors' roles and responsibilities—and even identities—changing under different ownership models. For instance, an AV owner may also be an AV operator when that company or person is offering rides for hire to customers/users. In this scenario, the customer/user also arguably could be considered the operator in that he or she decides on the destination. Another permutation could have a manufacturer retaining ownership of an AV and leasing it to a third-party operator, who, in turn, provides rides to customers/users. ZipCar illustrates an aspect of this potential future, where maintenance and (partial) insurance are bundled into the rental cost, but the fueling activity is a shared responsibility requiring the labor of the operator (who is also a customer/user), with payment being made by the owner.

The question of unlicensed drivers as customers/users of AVs further illustrates how current concepts of roles and responsibilities for all stakeholders across all phases of the vehicle life cycle may change. For instance, when AVs do not require a licensed driver in the car, manufacturers may need to change their assumptions for how the vehicle may be used. They may also need to change vehicle documentation, including owner's manuals. They cannot assume that the customer/user (who, as noted, may also be considered an operator in some scenarios) has the same knowledge base and experience as customers/users of current vehicles. In terms of information assurance, the presence of a person in the car cannot presume that person's ability to detect vehicle failure due to cyberattack. Indeed, a rideshare passenger could be oblivious to a hack of a car in which they were riding.

Myriad other factors may affect the role of the customer/user and the information assurance responsibilities of manufacturers, owners, and operators as AV design changes the riding experience. The potential to provide customized entertainment experiences to customers/users through the interior cabin design creates new cyber risks. For instance, a rider may want to be served up their favorite Netflix series when they enter an on-demand AV. That would imply that the owner or operator of the car has or gains possession of the customer/user's Netflix profile preferences. That information would be susceptible to hacking and would require cyber defenses. Likewise, custom content delivery may introduce the risk of targeted fraudulent sales pitches or opportunities to use messaging to spearphish customers/users who take advantage of interactive communications on board AVs. Finally, at the end of an AV's service life, stored data cannot be left unlocked prior to destruction or resale of the vehicle. This concern is a bookend to the concern of information assurance during recurring hand-offs of on-demand AVs across riders, whose data (e.g., profile preferences) might be retained for future rides.

### *Service Providers*

We also must project a future for service providers (e.g., maintenance shops) throughout the transportation service life phase. Because fewer AV customers/users are presumed to play a role in maintenance or operational security (because they lack the knowledge, ownership interest, or ability to do so), the demand for automated maintenance and software updates will increase. Thus, sites where automated, over-the-air maintenance takes place (e.g., individual driveways, parking lots with electric vehicle charging stations, gas stations) create opportunities for targeted cyber exploits that would have to be defended against, presumably by the party responsible for the maintenance (Table 5.4).

### *Future Considerations*

The potential changes in vehicle use will affect allocation of roles and responsibilities for information assurance in the service life phase.

**Table 5.4**
**Expansion of Responsibility in the Transportation Service Life Phase**

| Stakeholder Role | Potential Expansion in Responsibility vis-à-vis Information Assurance |
|---|---|
| Owner/operator | • Shared or consolidated maintenance roles for cyber protection<br>• User profile data protection or destruction |
| Customer/user | • Monitoring of unsafe software applications or marketing fraud in vehicle |
| Service providers (repair shops/services) | • Cyber protection of repair service facilities |

While this analysis does not make specific predictions, the future of AVs is likely to unfold in many unexpected ways for stakeholders.

Maintenance of the vehicle chassis and mechanical parts may continue in the same way as we know it today, while "smart," network-enabled electronic components may require new maintenance models. Thus, information assurance roles and responsibilities could reside with the party best positioned to steward each of those components.

Also, enhanced safety from the predicted reduction in vehicle crashes in an AV future could spur innovations such as inexpensive, plastic-frame cars, drastically reducing vehicle cost. In this eventuality, the replacement value of vehicles would decline, which might spur reconsideration of the criticality of cyber protection based on cost of repair, damage to property, and physical harms. Vehicle insurers base decisions on whether to repair or replace a damaged vehicle on its value. The cost of a cyber protection strategy will need to be balanced against the vehicle's worth or the exposure to risks of property damage, physical injury, and fatality. We build on this in our discussion of the market protection phase.

### Phase 4: Market Protection

The current market is structured to deal with human error as well as infrastructure deficits and mechanical defects. Vehicle regulations, including registration, inspection, and recalls, have adjusted to different road use patterns and safety changes. AVs and the new models of car ownership they may portend may change the roles of insurers, regulators, the government, and society.

We will focus on three stakeholders from the NIST CPS framework for this phase:

- service providers (lawyers and insurers)
- government/regulators
- the public.

### *Service Providers: Lawyers and Insurers*

The civil justice system plays a role in the determination of liability after motor vehicle collisions resulting in claims arising from damages, injury, and/or death. A future of cyberattacks on AVs will require expansion of legal precedents and strategies to respond to damages due to cyber vulnerabilities in AVs or smart infrastructure. Indeed, harms may not even involve a collision. Today, in many non-driving contexts, information assurance seeks to reduce the risk of losing control of sensitive, personal data. Thus, if information hacked from AV systems results in damage to users' finances, reputation, or career, then auto liability might come to encompass aspects of privacy law.

The automotive insurance industry is actively evaluating existing risk mitigation frameworks. The NHTSA and the Insurance Institute for Highway Safety have vehicle rating systems that focus on crashworthiness, but AVs may require regulators to establish regimes to test "cyberworthiness." That in turn may affect insurers' approaches to rate setting. In terms of insurer business models and coverages, present offers for "pay as you go" insurance coverage may initially expand in market share in a future of AVs if users require only intermittent coverage. Later, if manufacturers retain ownership of AVs (e.g., those that are used in rideshares), the focus of insurance may change to cover manufacturers and ride-sharing companies as owners in the absence of an owner/driver.

### *Regulators*

A possible shift of vehicle ownership from individuals to fleets in an era of AVs may change vehicle registration and inspection roles among components of the DOT (i.e., the Federal Motor Carrier Safety

Administration and NHTSA). It remains to be seen how rule-making at the state and federal levels will guide requirements for people who continue to drive, the transportation service providers responsible for registering and inspecting their fleets of AVs, and the AV users/consumers who may still need to demonstrate some form of training in lieu of driver licensing. Striking a proper balance between state regulation and federal oversight will only increase in importance going forward, while questions are already being asked regarding the harmonization of regulation across state lines (Eno Center for Transportation, 2017).

Where technological developments free riders from maintenance or operation of the vehicles, regulators may need to consider what consumer protections are appropriate to fit the changed circumstances. Indeed, the consequences of cyberattack to an automated driving system might resemble the existing risks presented by impairment of human drivers due to road rage, fatigue, alcohol abuse, use of illegal substances, side effects of medications, aggravation of medical impairments, or disability. Cyber exploits could make vehicles unable to see, understand, remember, or communicate. Establishing statutory regimes to protect or compensate AV users who suffer harms due to those cyber exploits may be more efficient than waiting for the civil justice system to develop case law adapted to the circumstances.

#### *The Public*

Assessing the role of the public in information assurance during the market protection phase must consider whether they are capable of performing the task (Table 5.5). That, in turn, will inform analysis of reasonableness standards. On the side of individual capability, training and certification options for AVs and their information assurance would be a question to explore. Scenarios where ownership of vehicles shifts toward fleets of on-demand AVs may alleviate individuals of such potential duties. Certainly, individual compliance with software configuration has been challenging in contexts such as cell phones. It is possible that the same issue will arise with AVs.

**Table 5.5**
**Expansion of Responsibility in the Market Protection Phase**

| Stakeholder Role | Expansion of Responsibility vis-à-vis Information Assurance |
|---|---|
| Service providers: lawyers | • Determining attribution and causation of cyberattack or exploit of vulnerability<br>• Added litigation of damages due to exposure of sensitive personal information |
| Service providers: insurers | • New vehicle safety/security certification requirements for coverage<br>• New user training/certification requirements for coverage<br>• Monitoring of vehicle use/control for billing period of insurance coverage<br>• Shifts in mix of insured parties and changes to risk mitigation framework |
| Government/ regulators | • Establishing standards for information sharing to support AVs sensing and communicating with infrastructure<br>• Setting new rules for vehicle safety/security certification<br>• Setting new rules for user training/certification<br>• Monitoring data sharing with infrastructure for connected vehicle risks<br>• Setting new vehicle safety/security certification policies<br>• Setting new user training/certification policies |
| The public | • Possible compliance with software configuration updates |

## Societal Perceptions and Responses to Emerging Autonomous Vehicle Trends

We have laid out how roles and responsibilities for information assurance may shift with the introduction of AVs and expansion of on-demand car services. We now focus more deeply on how people may respond to these changes, as those responses may inform the behavior of stakeholders in each of the four phases of an AV's life cycle.

### Perceptions and Social Response Related to Phase 1: Development and Production

For manufacturers, a strong selling point to automation is the potential for enhanced safety. The dilemma is that automated safety features can become a security threat in a world of AV hackers (SAE International, undated). Thus, exploits of a vulnerability to connected and automated systems present a security threat layered upon desirable safety control systems.

The public may not want improvements in vehicle, road, and transportation safety to come with added risk to their privacy or other aspects of their personal security. Some might argue that trading reduced risk from deaths in automobiles for new cyber risks is not acceptable. For manufacturers, the challenge is to demonstrate that the inherent risks of AVs are lower than those of conventional vehicles. Designing vehicle testing and validation programs for transparency to the public may enable greater dialogue and societal understanding of the trade-offs.

### Perceptions and Social Response Related to Phase 2: Market Offering

Over the life of a vehicle under the traditional model, stakeholders have had a largely linear sequence of handoffs in terms of roles and responsibilities. Manufacturers designed and produced cars, dealers sold cars, consumers purchased cars, and service providers (such as insurers) offered market protections. Under the emerging model of on-demand vehicles and shared rides, travelers only pay for a vehicle and insurance while they are using it. Thus, the point of sale is no longer a fixed dealership. That changes the touchpoints and interactions between the public and other stakeholders in the market offering phase. For example, with regard to information assurance risks, a compromised AV could record a user's trips and reveal substantial personal information about that individual. Any damages resulting from that vulnerability would alter the perceptions that the AV-purchasing public has of the dealer or ride-share operator.

### Perceptions and Social Response Related to Phase 3: Transportation Service Life

Currently, owners are responsible for routine maintenance (e.g., oil changes) and repairs over the life of the car or until it gets sold. Careful consideration will be needed to decide how this division of responsibilities extends to information assurance and cybersecurity measures. The service tasks of oil change, brake job, and tire rotation may provide a potential analogy to software updates and sensor maintenance in an AV. The role of cyber threat awareness and mitigation training will need to be carefully considered and allocated between fleet owners, transportation service providers, individual owners, and customers/users. The extent of potential disruption by cyberattacks means that some party or parties must assure the integrity of all data communications within vehicle systems, between vehicles, and across other nodes of communication.

Whether the existing responsibilities carry forward in the same way will depend on the nature of stakeholder relationships when fewer people own vehicles. Where people embrace a life without car ownership, AV on-demand services may feel like any other service offered by the retail or hospitality industry. Not only will the trim level of the car be a price differentiator when a customer seeks to buy an AV or choose a ride-share AV, but information assurance may also play into their decisions.[2]

### Perceptions and Social Response Related to Phase 4: Market Protections

In the regulatory arena, NHTSA provides federal guidance regarding cybersecurity best practices for modern vehicles and emphasizes greater specificity regarding the role of designers, manufacturers, suppliers, and maintainers (NHTSA, 2016a). Beyond these communities, the guidance supports educational efforts for nontechnical individuals and the stewardship of aftermarket devices. As vehicle maintenance and service relationships evolve, the guidance states that individuals and authorized third parties should not be unduly restricted. Much conversation and effort will be required to understand the balance of responsibilities across these stakeholder groups.

As to insurers in the age of AVs, consumer expectations and understanding of coverages for vehicle damages and medical treatment will need to be clarified. If transportation becomes more like the health care and financial industries, there will be very different expec-

---

[2] Anecdotally, it appears that relatively few consumers prioritize information security when making their decisions.

tations on how losses and damages are accounted for. While insurance norms like deductibles could remain part of the insurance model, other models exist. For example, banks that issue credit cards typically reimburse the customer for the costs of theft and fraudulent activities. If auto insurance policies are not designed for unlicensed "motorists" who would occupy AVs, then the public perception might be that all should be covered in the way that a contract of carriage is provided in the aviation industry.

## Future Considerations for Autonomous Vehicle Stakeholders

The spread of AV technology will change relationships between parties with respect to manufacture, distribution, ownership, use, and market protection of cars. Current roles and responsibilities may or may not strongly inform how responsibility for information assurance will evolve. On the whole, our analysis suggests that the roles of many stakeholders for information assurance of AVs will likely lengthen and intensify compared with their current statuses. Thus, stakeholders may have to take steps to meet these intensified, extended responsibilities.

Additional future considerations for stakeholders in the AV future are as follows:

- **AV users:** For AV users, automated safety features will reduce crash risks, although the information assurance risks they face will expand. Accordingly, for manufacturers, vehicle performance testing may extend from rating crashworthiness to include rating how well AVs resist hacks, although this may prove difficult in practice.
- **Policymakers:** Policymakers will have to allocate responsibilities for vehicle monitoring, either by training the public to detect and avert hacks or by motivating public compliance with corporate monitoring of their activities. Alternatively, responsibility for monitoring will have to reside with other stakeholders, such

as manufacturers, repair facilities, or providers of on-demand AV services.

- **Corporate AV owners:** The potential for hacks on operators of AV fleets appears to support corporate monitoring of systems, rather than monitoring by individuals, to prevent and mitigate harms. Part of that system should include feedback channels for the public to share ways that cyberattacks can be detected as the technologies mature.
- **Manufacturer/supply chain:** Integration of new features by manufacturers for existing models (to be installed via software update) and add-on software products by aftermarket suppliers will require tight coordination to preserve information assurance.

CHAPTER SIX

# Civil Liability and Cyberattacks: General Legal Framework

Our analysis has described how AVs work and the connected roadway infrastructure they are likely to inhabit. We have documented the avenues that hackers could use to gain access to AV systems and the kinds of hacks they could perpetrate, as well as the potential for those hacks to cause damage in the real world. Next, we consider the civil legal framework into which the AV industry will launch. As later substantiated in this chapter, we observe that it is likely that existing civil liability law is sufficiently flexible to adapt to hacked AV liability claims as state and federal law and regulations evolve to create a policy framework around the technology.

This chapter outlines the general legal framework for civil liability after a cyberattack on an AV. First, we will discuss the circumstances under which a party may be held civilly liable for the criminal acts of a third party. For the purposes of this discussion, we assume that the party responsible for the attack is not identified. Next, we discuss the distinction between purely economic losses (e.g., lost profits) and other types of harms (e.g., personal injury and damage to other property) that can result from a cyberattack. We then discuss which party or parties (e.g., vehicle manufacturers, software companies) are likely to be named as defendants in the event of a lawsuit arising from a cyberattack on an AV. We also summarize recent statements by AV manufacturers concerning acceptance of liability.

We discuss federal and state laws that specifically apply to AVs. As further detailed in this chapter, because there are very few federal and state laws on autonomous and connected vehicles, legal commentators and policy researchers have concluded that traditional product liability laws are likely to govern in the event of civil lawsuits arising from AV crashes. The product liability theories outlined by these commentators and researchers, along with warranty law and state and federal privacy laws, are likely to be the most relevant body of law in lawsuits arising specifically from cyberattacks on AVs.

We also provide a brief overview of the civil liability that may result from defective software, as that discussion may provide relevant analogies to claims against makers of AV software. As detailed below, although vendors of defective software have used the economic loss rule and the Uniform Commercial Code (UCC) to shield themselves from legal liability, vendors of software incorporated in AVs will likely be subject to traditional product liability theories because software incorporated in autonomous vehicles will lead to noneconomic losses—i.e., damages to persons and property.

In the last half of this chapter, we discuss how civil liability theories, warranty law, and privacy law will apply in cases involving cyberattacks on AVs.

## Civil Liability for the Criminal Actions of Another Party

This report focuses on civil liability issues that manufacturers, distributors, and drivers of AVs will face after a cyberattack. Still, it is worth noting that if perpetrators of cyberattacks are identified and arrested, they are likely to be subject to traditional state and federal criminal laws. For example, if a cyberattack results in death, the hacker may face manslaughter or murder charges (Gurney, 2015).

An AV hacker might also face criminal penalties under federal statutes, such as the Electronic Communications Privacy Act, 18 U.S.C. §§ 2510–2511 (2012) (ECPA);[1] the Computer Fraud and Abuse

[1] The ECPA prohibits interception, use, disclosure, and procurement of wire, oral, and electronic communications.

Act, 18 U.S.C. § 1030 (1984);[2] the Digital Millennium Copyright Act (1998);[3] the Wiretap Act, 18 U.S.C. § 2511 (1968);[4] and potentially the USA PATRIOT Act (Kohler and Colbert-Taylor, 2014).[5] A hacker might also face civil liability under intentional tort theories, such as trespass to chattels or intentional infliction of emotional distress. However, historically, it is very difficult to identify and apprehend individuals responsible for a particular attack. As a result, this section focuses on parties that are likely to be named as defendants in a civil lawsuit.

Generally, a party will not be held civilly liable for the criminal acts of a third party unless the party could have (1) reasonably foreseen the criminal act and (2) prevented it. One authority refers to this liability determination principle as the "foreseeability/capacity analysis," in which "the degree of foreseeability is balanced against the level of capacity to act" (Tuck, 2013). Similarly, in *Lille v. Thompson*, the U.S. Supreme Court recognized a duty to protect against foreseeable criminal acts by third parties.[6] The U.S. Supreme Court found that whether "[t]he foreseeable danger was from intentional or criminal misconduct is irrelevant; respondent nonetheless had a duty to make reasonable provision against it. Breach of that duty would be negligence."[7]

State courts have also recognized a duty to protect against criminal acts, but again only when such criminal acts are foreseeable. For

---

[2] The Computer Fraud and Abuse Act prohibits accessing a computer without authorization.

[3] The Digital Millennium Copyright Act criminalizes production and dissemination of technology intended to circumvent measures that control access to copyrighted works (e.g., security systems).

[4] The Wiretap Act protects the privacy of wire and oral communications.

[5] Among other things, the USA PATRIOT Act gives law enforcement agencies broad powers to investigate potential terrorist threats and provides for increased penalties for convicted terrorists.

[6] In *Lille*, the plaintiff worked as a night-shift telegraph operator in an isolated building that was poorly lit, not guarded or patrolled, and located in an area frequented by "dangerous characters." The plaintiff was required to open a door multiple times each night to pass messages to other employees, and she was unable determine who was at the door without unlocking it. One night, a third party forced the door open after the plaintiff opened it and attacked the plaintiff (*Lille v. Thompson*, 332 U.S. 459, 1947).

[7] *Lille v. Thompson*, 1947, pp. 461–462.

example, Georgia's Supreme Court has held that "[a] landlord's duty to exercise ordinary care to protect tenants against third-party criminal attacks extends only to foreseeable criminal acts."[8]

The duty to protect against a foreseeable criminal act is not absolute. A defendant only has a duty to take *reasonable* steps to protect against harm. In other words, in determining whether a defendant had a duty to protect against a criminal act, courts balance the defendant's capacity to prevent the harm against the foreseeability of the criminal act. For example, in *Ann M. v. Pacific Plaza Shopping Center*,[9] the court determined whether a commercial lessor breached a duty to an employee of a lessee to protect against criminal activity. The plaintiff employee was attacked while working in the leased premises and argued that the commercial lessor breached its duty by not hiring private security guards after transients had been spotted on the premises. Balancing foreseeability and costs, the California Supreme Court held that no such duty was owed.

In short, if a party fails to take reasonable precautions to protect against the criminal acts of a third party under this foreseeability/capacity analysis, the party may be held liable under a negligence theory. However, in balancing competing interests, the social costs of imposing a duty must be taken into account. In the following discussion of civil liability theories, we cover negligence in greater detail. As illustrated in the case law discussed in this section, because of the role of foreseeability in determinations of liability for the criminal acts of a third party, the issue of prior exploitation of a vulnerability of a component part or system in the AV will likely play an important role in liability determinations.

---

[8] *Sturbridge Partners Ltd. v. Walker*, 482 S.E.2d 339, 340, Ga., 1997. The Louisiana Court of Appeal similarly held that

> the duty to protect business patrons does not extend to the unforeseeable or unanticipated criminal acts of an independent third person. Only when the owner or management of a business has knowledge, or can be imputed with knowledge, of a third person's intended criminal conduct which is about to occur, and which is within the power of the owner or management to protect against, does such a duty of care towards a guest arise (*Davenport v. Nixon*, 434 So. 2d 1203, 1205, La. Ct. App., 1983).

[9] *Ann M. v. Pacific Plaza Shopping Center*, 863 P.2d 207, Cal., 1993.

## The Economic Loss Rule

In our discussion of the tort theories of negligence and strict liability, the distinction between purely economic damages and other damages is important. Under the economic loss rule, a party who suffers only economic harm may only recover damages under a contract theory, as opposed to a tort theory (such as strict liability and negligence, discussed below).[10] Purely economic harm caused by a product is harm that does not result in personal injury or damage to property other than the product itself.[11] For example, XYZ company buys a conveyer belt from ABC company and XYZ loses production time when launching its new model because the conveyer belt malfunctions. Shutting down production causes XYZ to lose millions of dollars in profit because the delay in production allows a rival company to market its new model a week before XYZ company. XYZ has suffered purely economic loss and cannot recover from ABC under a tort cause of action.[12] However, the economic loss rule does not bar recovery of economic damages resulting from personal injury or damage to property other than the product itself. For example, if a defective product results in personal injury, then lost wages and medical bills arising from the personal injury are not barred by the economic loss rule.[13] If a defective car blows up and damages a house, the owner of the house may recover damages in tort and is not barred by the economic loss rule because the damage sustained was damage to property other than the defective product itself.[14] The distinction between purely economic loss, which can only be recovered under a contract theory, and damages that may be recovered under a tort theory is important because tort claims pro-

---

[10] Johnson, 2009.

[11] *Am. Aviation*, 891 So. 2d, 2004, pp. 538–541 (limiting the economic loss rule to circumstances where the parties are either in contractual privity or the defendant is a manufacturer or distributor of a product, and no established exception to the application of the rule applies).

[12] Restatement (Third) of Torts: Prods. Liab. § 21, 1997, cmt. d, illus. 3.

[13] Sawaya, 2014.

[14] Sawaya, 2014.

vide at least three advantages over claims based in contract law (Sawaya, 2014, p. 1084). First, recovery under a contract theory is limited to reasonably foreseeable damages resulting from a breach of contractual duties. Tort claims allow for recovery for damages proximately caused by a defendant's tortuous conduct. Second, for the purposes of statutes of limitation under tort theories, the clock does not begin to run until the plaintiff knew or should have known of their injury. Third, the standard of proof to recover under a contract theory is more rigorous (Sawaya, 2014). As will be further discussed in the "Civil Liability Theories" section, negligence and strict liability theories will likely play important roles in lawsuits arising from cyberattacks on AVs. Bear in mind that purely economic losses cannot be recovered under negligence and strict liability theories.

## Potential Defendants

As illustrated in our earlier discussion of the types of damage that might be wreaked by a hacked AV and the NIST CPS framework, an array of defendants may face liability claims. To focus this analysis of liability for hacked AVs, we will narrow our consideration to a few of those entities: car manufacturers, software manufacturers, AV distributors, and AV owners and operators.

Legal commentators analyzing the issue of which parties are likely to be named as defendants in lawsuits arising from AV crashes have argued that for "practical and doctrinal" reasons, manufacturers of AVs are the parties most likely to be named as defendants and held liable for incidents involving the vehicles (Anderson et al., 2016; Kalra, Anderson, and Wachs, 2009).[15] First, car manufacturers have historically had significant assets. Second, "the vehicle manufacturer, as the party ultimately responsible for the final product, will be the most likely party

[15] See also Marchant and Lindor, 2012; Duffy and Hopkins, 2013; Funkhouser, 2013; Garza, 2012; Glancy, Peterson, and Graham, 2016; Graham, 2012; Gurney, 2013; Hubbard, 2014; Mele, 2013; Swanson, 2014; Vladeck, 2014; Wu, 2015; Gasser, 2012; Roberts et al., 1993; and Villasenor, 2014.

to be found liable" (Marchant and Lindor, 2012). With respect to the second point, Marchant and Lindor (2012) notes:

> [T]he manufacturer of a component part is not liable for defects in the final product over which it had not control, although it is liable if the part was defective when the component left the manufacturer. A similar rule is likely to apply to the software engineer. So, unless the component part or software engineer produced a product that was clearly defective, the vehicle manufacturer will be the party most likely to be fingered for liability, although there will likely be cases where other parties are sued.[16]

However, many of these commentators' conclusions are based on cases involving conventional vehicles. In the future, the tendency of vehicle manufacturers to bear responsibility for crashes may change if (1) the AV manufacturer is a relatively small start-up and/or (2) the software manufacturer has deep pockets and seems more responsible. For example, if an AV is running Waymo software and crashes as a result of a software problem, a plaintiff will likely sue Waymo and the AV manufacturer. Marchant and Lindor (2012) notes that "unless the component part or software engineer produced a product that was clearly defective, the vehicle manufacturer is likely to bear liability." However, by their very nature, cyberattacks exploit specific vulnerabilities in specific products. Although locating the vulnerability in the AV system may require significant expertise and expenditure, it will likely be possible—at least in some instances—to locate specific flaws in specific components or software. Thus, in lawsuits arising from cyberattacks on AVs, a range of defendants—including AV manufacturers, software companies, AV distributers, and AV drivers—may be named. There may be contractual indemnification provisions and related pro-

---

[16] Marchant and Lindor (2012) cites Restatement (Third) of Torts: Product Liability § 5 cmt. b (1997):

> The component seller is required to provide instructions and warnings regarding risks associated with the use of the component product. However, when a sophisticated buyer integrates a component into another product, the component seller owes no duty to warn either the immediate buyer or ultimate consumers of dangers arising because the component is unsuited for the special purpose to which the buyer puts it.

tections in contracts between AV manufacturers and component part manufacturers. In these instances, if a component part is defective and causes damage, the manufacturer of the component part would be required to indemnify the AV manufacturer.

State and municipal transportation departments might also face liability. As noted in a 2016 Transportation Research Board report on the legal environment for driverless cars (Glancy, Peterson, and Graham, 2016), the connected vehicle environment may rely more heavily on communications between AVs and roadside infrastructure than experts currently anticipate. This would require significant municipal and state engagement in infrastructure development, which would open the door for negligence claims against state and local authorities (Glancy, Peterson, and Graham, 2016). This potential liability may explain state and municipalities' reluctance to participate in infrastructure development. Although potential government liability for negligence in infrastructure development is beyond the scope of this report, we discuss the issue of government liability in Chapter Seven (Scenario 3).

## Acceptance of Liability by Autonomous Vehicle Manufacturers

Some AV manufacturers may accept liability when their cars are in autonomous mode, but it is unclear whether such assumption of liability will hold in the case of a cyberattack.[17] The extent and strength of

[17] In 2015, Volvo Car Group President and CEO Håkan Samuelsson stated that Volvo will assume all liability when its vehicles are in autonomous mode (Korosec, 2015). Mercedes-Benz and Google reportedly made similar commitments to accept liability for crashes involving their autonomous cars, if their technology is at fault (Risen, 2015). As of 2015, GM declined to make a public statement regarding liability for autonomous vehicles. GM spokesman Dan Flores stated, "We do have an increasing number of automated and driver assistance features in our cars, but the driver is still in control and is still ultimately responsible" (Korosec, 2015). Ford Motor Co. spokesman Alan Hall similarly declined to publicly announce Ford's position on accepting liability for AVs. The head of the NHTSA welcomed commitments by AV manufacturers to accept liability for accidents involving their vehicles when their technology is at fault, noting that such commitment will hasten distribution

commitments to accept liability will likely not be tested until AVs are commercially distributed and a cyberattack resulting from a vulnerability in the manufacturer's technology occurs.

## Federal and State Laws and Best Practices Relating to Autonomous Vehicles

In September 2016, DOT issued, as agency guidance, its initial *Federal Automated Vehicles Policy* pertaining to both highly automated vehicles and lesser-automated vehicles (DOT, 2016). In September 2017, DOT issued *Automated Driving Systems 2.0: Vision for Safety* (DOT, 2017), an updated version of the *Federal Automated Vehicles Policy*. *Automated Driving Systems 2.0* emphasizes the voluntary nature of the policy and modifies the list of safety elements issued in the 2016 version. And, on October 4, 2018, DOT issued *Preparing for the Future of Transportation: Automated Vehicles 3.0.* These publications are meant to help entities engaged in testing and deployment identify and resolve safety issues before deployment. One of the 12 safety elements is cybersecurity. Under this element, DOT (2017) encourages entities

> to consider and incorporate voluntary guidance, best practices, and design principles published by National Institute of Standards and Technology (NIST21), NHTSA, SAE International, the Alliance of Automobile Manufacturers, the Association of Global Automakers, the Automotive Information Sharing and Analysis Center (Auto-ISAC), and other relevant organizations, as appropriate.

*Automated Driving Systems 2.0* also clarifies the differences in federal and state authority and their roles in establishing safety practices and recommends best practices for state legislatures developing AV regulations (DOT, 2017). Although the guidance in all three versions of

---

of AVs (Korosec, 2015). However, statements by Volvo, Mercedes, and Google regarding acceptance of liability do not make clear whether such acceptance extends to cyberattack incidents.

*Automated Driving Systems* is nonbinding and voluntary, courts may consider the "voluntary guidance, best practices, and design principles" referenced under the cybersecurity element when determining whether an AV manufacturer or a manufacturer of a component part or system complied with industry standards and best practices (as further discussed in the "Negligence" subsection of the "Civil Liability Theories" section and in Scenario 1 in Chapter Seven).

However, developing best practices for cybersecurity has been challenging in other fields. Adherence to a single set of best practices also risks "monoculture"—that a single "solution" to cybersecurity will emerge. Paradoxically, this may make systems more vulnerable if a determined hacker (e.g., a nation state) is able to identify a vulnerability.

State law on autonomous and connected vehicles is developing, but the majority of states do not have any laws on autonomous and connected vehicles. According to the National Conference of State Legislatures' online Autonomous Vehicle State Bill Tracking Database (National Conference of State Legislatures, 2018), as of September 2018, 21 states have pending or enacted laws on autonomous and connected vehicles. In addition, one federal bill relating to AVs is currently under consideration (the Autonomous Vehicle Privacy Protection Act of 2015), and another bill has been enacted (the Fixing America's Surface Transportation [FAST] Act).[18] Notably, under the Model State Policy section of DOT's 2017 *Automated Driving Systems 2.0*, DOT recommended that "[s]etting Federal Motor Vehicle Safety Standards (FMVSSs) for new motor vehicles and motor vehicle equipment (with which manufacturers must certify compliance before they sell their vehicles)" and "[e]nforcing compliance with FMVSSs" should be federal responsibilities.

In the absence of federal and state laws governing civil liability for AV-related incidents, traditional product liability laws will likely apply, as detailed in the remainder of this chapter.

---

[18] Stanford University's Center for Internet and Society maintains a wiki that tracks legislative and regulatory developments related to automated driving, automatic driving, autonomous driving, self-driving vehicles, and driverless cars (Weiner and Smith, 2017).

## Liability for Software Flaws

As Geistfeld (2017) notes, "there is no established body of case law recognizing that a manufacturer incurs a tort duty for defective software." Historically, most lawsuits in which plaintiffs have sought to hold software vendors liable for defective or insecure software have been unsuccessful (Scott, 2008). Because courts consider software to be a good rather than a service, these claims are typically governed by the UCC (Scott, 2008). Article 2 of the UCC permits warranty disclaimers, and software vendors typically disclaim warranties. Scott (2008) noted that no reported decision has unequivocally held that a software vendor has breached an express warranty because (1) software manufacturers are careful to avoid making any promises that their software will perform particular tasks, (2) licensing agreements usually disclaim any express promises, and (3) it is generally accepted that software will not perform perfectly (Scott, 2008). Courts also tend to uphold implied warranty disclaimers unless such disclaimers are found to be unconscionable. Software vendors also limit their liability and potential plaintiffs' remedies through contractual clauses, such as liquidated damages provisions and provisions that limit remedies to repair and replacement of defective parts or limit damages to direct damages (and exclude special, incidental, and consequential damages) (Scott, 2008).

As Geistfeld (2017) and Scott (2008) note, although product liability law would seem to provide an alternate theory for plaintiffs, the economic loss rule and contractual disclaimers tend to preclude product liability claims against software vendors. Defective software usually results in lost or corrupted data, lost employee time, and remediation costs. These losses "fall within the economic loss doctrine and cannot be recovered in a product liability action" (Neuburger and Garde, 2004) because they "stem from the alleged failure of the computer system to perform as expected and not from injury to another person or property."[19] Another major impediment is the fact that, in

---

[19] *Krider Pharmacy & Gifts, Inc. v. Medi-Care Data Sys., Inc.*, 791 F. Supp. 221, 226, E.D. Wis., 1992.

the commercial context, the UCC displaces tort liability with respect to property damage (Scott, 2008).

However, as noted in Rustad and Koenig (2005) (an article on tort liability for cybercrime), courts regularly impose liability where defective software causes physical injury. For example, in *General Motors Corp. v. Johnston*, a Chevrolet pickup truck stalled in an intersection and was struck by a logging truck, killing the passenger in the pickup truck. A defective computer chip that controlled the fuel delivery system caused the pickup truck to stall, and there was evidence that GM was aware of the stalling problem in its pickup trucks but did not take remedial action to protect drivers.[20] Plaintiffs brought product liability claims, and, at trial, the jury found in favor of the plaintiffs. The Supreme Court of Alabama affirmed the judgment of the trial court. In *Corley v. Stryker Corp.*, during the plaintiff's knee replacement surgery, her surgeon used ShapeMatch Cutting Guide software manufactured by Stryker Orthopaedics to guide the marking of the bone before cutting. The plaintiff alleged that she suffered pain, discomfort, joint instability, limited mobility, and knee misalignment after surgery. The ShapeMatch Cutting Guide software used by the plaintiff's surgeon was recalled four years after the plaintiff's surgery. The plaintiff brought suit under tort theories against Stryker Orthopaedics. In denying Stryker Orthopaedics' motion to dismiss, the court found that the plaintiff's allegations that the software was defective "sufficiently alleged that the cutting guide used during [the plaintiff's] surgery was unreasonably dangerous in design due to the alleged software defects" and could sustain a products liability claim.[21] In *In re Air Crash Near Cali, Colombia on December 20, 1995*, flaws in software were found to be partly responsible for the crash of American Airlines Flight 965. The crash was caused in part by the poor design of the navigational database programmed into the flight management computer. Plaintiffs in the lawsuit alleged that defendants concealed code problems (Sundvall

---

20 *General Motors Corp. v. Johnston*, 592 So. 2d 1054, Ala., 1992.

21 *Corley v. Stryker Corp.*, No. 6:13-CV-02571, 2014 WL 3375596 at *1, W.D. La, May 27, 2014, adopted; *Corley v. Stryker Orthopaedics*, No. 13-2571, 2014 WL 3125990, W.D. La., July 3, 2014. See Beck and Jacobson, 2017.

and Andolina, 2000). They brought claims against American Airlines for negligence.[22] They also brought claims against Honeywell, Inc. (the supplier of the aircraft's flight management computer) and Jeppesen Sanderson, Inc. (the provider of the navigational database programmed into the flight management computer and the corresponding aviation charts) for negligence, strict liability, intentional misrepresentation, negligent misrepresentation, and fraudulent concealment.[23] A federal jury in the Southern District of Florida decided that American Airlines was 75 percent at fault for the crash, Jeppesen was 17 percent at fault, and Honeywell was 8 percent at fault. The jury found Jeppesen and Honeywell liable because they accepted American Airlines' claim that Jeppesen and Honeywell fraudulently concealed a problem with the database.

As indicated by courts' willingness to allow plaintiffs who suffered physical injuries to bring claims against manufacturers of allegedly defective software, manufacturers of software incorporated in AV systems and the manufacturers of the AV systems will likely be subject to traditional product liability theories. Defects in this software will lead to noneconomic losses (damages to persons and property), and thus these manufacturers will not be shielded by the economic loss rule. Indeed, in contemplating liability for flaws in software associated with AVs, Geistfeld (2017) concludes,

> The rationale for the tort obligation . . . is much more straightforward in the case of autonomous vehicles. The coding or design of the operating system determines the performance of a product—a motor vehicle. Although the coding is an intangible form of intellectual property developed for a specific purpose, these are not sufficient reasons for eliminating the tort duty. If they were, then a conventional motor vehicle that performs according to engineering plans that were developed or otherwise embodied in a computer program would also be exempt from tort liability.

---

[22] *In re Air Crash Near Cali, Colombia on December 20, 1995*, 985 F. Supp. 1106, S.D. Fla, 1997.

[23] *Tafuri v. Jeppesen Sanderson, Inc.*, 25 F. Supp. 2d 1364, Dist. Court, S.D. Fla., 1998.

## Civil Liability Theories

Public policy researchers and legal commentators—including Kalra, Anderson, and Wachs (2009), Anderson et al. (2016), Glancy (2015), Kohler and Colbert-Taylor (2014), and Villasenor (2014)—have catalogued civil liability theories that are likely to be generally relevant in incidents involving AVs. Below, we summarize the legal theories identified by these researchers and commentators and discuss how these theories might apply in cases involving cyberattacks on AVs.

### Negligence

In the context of cyberattacks on AVs, negligence will likely play a prominent role in civil liability determinations. Parties injured by cyberattacks may bring negligence claims against manufacturers, distributors, and sellers of AVs and component parts. These claims would be based on allegations that defendants failed to exercise reasonable care in the production, distribution, or sale of an AV or component part. Injured parties might also bring negligence claims against owners or users of an AV, based on allegations that owners or users failed to exercise reasonable care in the operation of an AV (e.g., an owner who rejects an important security update). In order to succeed on a negligence claim, a plaintiff would have to prove (1) a duty owed by defendant to plaintiff, (2) breach of the duty, (3) causation (i.e., breach of the duty caused some type of noneconomic injury to plaintiff), and (4) damages. Below, we discuss each of these elements and note issues that might arise under each of these elements in the cyberattack context.

#### *Duty*

Historically, "[c]ourts will find a duty where, in general, reasonable persons would recognize it and agree that it exists."[24] In the context of AVs, we anticipate that courts will readily find that likely defendants had a duty to likely injured plaintiffs. Software vendors, original equipment manufacturers, suppliers, and government agencies are all likely

---

[24] Prosser and Keeton, 1984, pp. 358–359.

to be found to have a duty to the users of AVs. The real question is likely to be whether that duty was breached.

### Breach of Duty

Courts have adopted three broad interpretations of reasonableness to determine whether the defendant breached its duty of reasonable care toward the plaintiff: (1) A court may compare the defendant's conduct to that of a hypothetical reasonable person who has "shortcomings that the community would tolerate but is otherwise a model of propriety and personifies the community ideal of appropriate behavior;" (2) a court may find a prima facie breach of duty if the defendant violated a statute; and (3) a court may undertake a cost-benefit analysis that examines the precautions a defendant could have taken but did not (de Villiers, 2004). In discussing breach of duty, we focus on the second interpretation (violation of a statute) and the third interpretation (cost-benefit analysis) because these standards are the ones most likely to be relevant in the cyberattack context. The cost-benefit analysis is the most commonly used standard in real-world settings. The rules of conduct and violation of a statute standards are relevant because many state and federal laws regarding AVs are currently under consideration.

#### Cost-Benefit Analysis

If a court adopted the commonly used cost-benefit analysis to determine whether a duty had been breached, a plaintiff would have to identify a precaution that each defendant could have taken to avoid the attack (e.g., the car manufacturer should have incorporated specific alternate technology to prevent the cyberattack) and show that the costs of adopting alternative technology that is less vulnerable to attacks or other precautionary measures are outweighed by the risks involved with not taking the measure. As Anderson et al. (2016) notes, the use of cost-benefit analysis to determine whether manufacturers are negligent will raise many complex questions. For example, when is the socially optimal time to release technology that will save lives if the technology can still be improved upon if its release is delayed? To illustrate this issue, Anderson et al. (2016) described a hypothetical crash involving a vehicle equipped with a crash-prevention system that operates successfully 70 percent of the time. However, the system could operate successfully 90 percent of the time if its release were delayed to permit additional development of the technology. If the 70-percent version of the system is released and a plaintiff is injured in a crash that would have been prevented if the 90-percent version of the system had been developed and released instead, should a court's analysis focus on the manufacturer's failure to develop the system that operated successfully 90 percent of the time? Can a manufacturer count the 70 percent of crashes that are avoided as a benefit of the technology? As Anderson et al. (2016) notes, allowing manufacturers to cite long-run benefits may encourage the adoption of life-saving technology but may shield the manufacturer from liability for shorter-run decisions that are inefficiently dangerous. Broader perspectives on benefits would assist AV and subsystem manufacturers because manufacturers could potentially count saved lives, avoided vehicle crashes, and/or reduction of air pollution among the positive aspects of AV technology.

Cost-benefit analysis would require the court to become familiar, through the use of experts, with the technology at issue and the costs of superior technology that would be less susceptible to this type of attack. To refer to a computer liability analogy that may inform hacked AV liability analysis, de Villiers (2004) notes that in the context of negligence claims arising from computer virus infection,

> Technology plays a crucial role in a negligence analysis involving virus infection. Courts require a plaintiff to prove breach of duty in a negligence action by identifying an untaken precaution and showing that the precaution would have yielded greater benefits in accident reduction than its cost. Such a cost-benefit analysis requires a familiarity with the technology as well as economics of viruses and virus detection.

In addition, in weighing costs of adopting specific alternative technologies or precautionary measures, courts would have to weigh the costs and benefits of preventing or minimizing the vulnerability not only in the AV that is the subject of a lawsuit but also in all similar AVs. As de Villiers (2004) notes in the computer virus context,

> A conventional hacker can destroy data worth, say, an amount D, releasing a virus to do the same job can cause this harm several times over by spreading into N systems, causing damage of magnitude N x D, where N can be very large. Although the two types of security breaches do similar damage in a particular computer, the virus's greater inherent danger is that it can multiply and repeat the destruction several times over.

### Rules of Conduct and Statutory Violation Standard

Violation of a law or an administrative regulation can also establish a prima facie breach of duty. For example, if the owner of a vehicle violates a law requiring that all cars in the jurisdiction have functioning headlights and the owner of the vehicle later hits a pedestrian because he was driving at night without headlights, a court may find that violation of the headlights law establishes a prima facie breach of duty. A 2015 article on the legal landscape that awaits AVs noted that, although "no security standards for first generation autonomous cars are yet in place," legal standards for both cybersecurity and privacy are currently being developed (Glancy, 2015). Once these legal standards are in place, a plaintiff may be able to identify a security standard breached by one or more of the defendants to establish a breach with respect to that defendant.

Courts will also likely start to take industry standards into account as AV technology progresses. Industry standards embody collective knowledge and customs within the relevant industry and can be introduced by a plaintiff to demonstrate that a defendant breached a standard of care in a negligence action:

> Industry customs are often developed over time and informally as a matter of trial and error by engineers working in the field. . . . Evidence of applicable customs may tend to show the foreseeability of the risk as well as the cost, feasibility, utility, and acceptability among consumers of the particular safety measures the plaintiff asserts the defendant negligently failed to adopt . . . (Owen, 2004).

Thus, as AV manufacturers develop customs with respect to minimizing vulnerability of parts and systems to cyberattacks, courts may take these customs into account when making negligence determinations. Formal industry standards may be given more weight by courts:

> Many formal product safety standards are promulgated by standard-setting organizations. . . . Because the organizations that issue such standards and codes may be heavily influenced (if not controlled) by industry, courts generally treat the admissibility of such standards the same as any other industry standards. But the formal way in which such standards may be developed and formulated into specific codes, and industry's commensurate reliance upon them, suggest that they sometimes should be accorded greater weight (Owen, 2004).

In this context, the auto industry's establishment of the Automotive Information Sharing and Analysis Center (Auto-ISAC) to develop and share cybersecurity best practices is relevant (Auto-ISAC, 2019). Once these standards are in place, plaintiffs in lawsuits arising from cyberattacks on AVs can offer these standards as evidence of a breach of the relevant standard of care.

However, unlike relevant statutes or administrative regulations (the violation of which can establish prima facie breach of duty), industry standards are not legally binding. As stated previously, DOT's *Automated Driving Systems 2.0* (DOT, 2017) encourages entities

> to consider and incorporate voluntary guidance, best practices, and design principles published by National Institute of Standards and Technology (NIST21), NHTSA, SAE International, the Alliance of Automobile Manufacturers, the Association of Global Automakers, the Automotive Information Sharing and Analysis Center (Auto-ISAC), and other relevant organizations, as appropriate.

Nonetheless, DOT's *Automated Driving Systems 2.0* (DOT, 2017) emphasizes the voluntary nature of the guidelines.

### *Causation*

In order to establish the causation element of a negligence cause of action, a plaintiff must prove cause-in-fact and proximate causation, as detailed below.

#### Cause-in-Fact

Most courts adopt the "but for" test. In other words, "but for" the defendant's negligence, the plaintiff would not have been injured. For example, if an AV hits a pedestrian after a hacker interferes with the vehicle's visual sensors, affecting its ability to spot obstructions, the pedestrian might bring a negligence claim against the owner of the vehicle. If it is discovered that the owner of the vehicle rejected an important security update, which would have prevented the cyberattack that interfered with the visual sensors, then a court would likely hold that the owner's negligence in rejecting the update was the cause-in-fact of the pedestrian's injury. However, if the rejection of the security update created a vulnerability in one of the AV's systems but did not affect the system that controlled the visual sensors, then cause-in-fact could not be established by pointing to the owner's rejection of the security update.

#### Proximate Causation

Proximate causation requires that a defendant's conduct be "reasonably related" to the plaintiff's harm in order for the defendant to be liable. In other words, the injury that occurred as a result of the defendant's conduct must be within the scope of reasonably foreseeable injury, and the plaintiff must be part of the class of persons who could be foreseeably injured by the defendant's conduct (de Villiers, 2004).

With respect to crashes that result solely from defective technology (i.e., when no third-party bad actor is involved), "[c]ourts have determined that automobile accidents are a reasonably foreseeable consequence of defective automated technology" (Wittenberg, 2016). However, when a third-party bad actor is involved, the issue of foreseeability is more complex. In the context of cyberattacks on AVs, the central question will be whether the injury caused by a third-party bad actor was a foreseeable result of defendant manufacturer or AV owner negligence. The third-party bad actor may have a "tendency to bond with trouble" because that actor is "shielded from liability by anonymity [or] insufficient assets" (de Villiers, 2004).

Examples of such bad actors include computer virus authors and hackers. In deciding whether to hold a defendant liable for a third-party bad actor's conduct, courts may consider whether the defendant created a foreseeable opportunity for the conduct. In *Stansbie v. Troman*, a court found the defendant liable under a negligence theory for the criminal acts of a third party.[25] The defendant was an interior designer who failed to lock the door of her client's house, thus allowing a burglar to enter the house and steal the client's jewelry. The court held that the defendant was liable for the homeowner's loss because the defendant created an opportunity for a criminal that would not have existed otherwise. De Villiers (2005) has applied this paradigm to the cyberattack context:

> The unlocked door provides additional encouragement to the bricks-and-mortar intruder by lowering his transactions costs. Analogously, security vulnerabilities lower the cyber attacker's transaction costs by making attacks faster and more efficient, conveniently remotely executable, and less likely to be blocked before substantial harm is done.

As noted above, because of the role of foreseeability in determinations of liability for the criminal acts of a third party, whether a similar attack (i.e., exploitation of a vulnerability of a component or system in the AV) has occurred in the past will likely play a key role in liability determinations.

### *Damages*

Damages are a relatively straightforward issue in the context of cyberattack on AVs when physical damage has occurred. For example, if a plaintiff proves that a cyberattack resulted in the disablement of the AV's brakes and a subsequent collision, a court would likely find that the plaintiff has established the damages element of the negligence claim.

---

[25] *Stansbie v. Troman*, 2 K.B. 48, 1948 (appeal taken from B.C.).

The issue of damages arising from unexploited vehicle attack vulnerabilities has already arisen in two cases. In *Cahen v. Toyota Motor Corp.*, filed in 2015, individuals who purchased Toyota, Ford, and GM cars alleged that a lack of security in the cars' computer systems allowed basic vehicle functions to be controlled by individuals outside the car, endangering vehicle occupants.[26] The district court dismissed the plaintiffs' claims, and the court of appeal upheld the dismissal. Although the plaintiffs did not include a cause of action for negligence, the district court rejected the damages theory associated with the plaintiffs' causes of action for violation of consumer protection statutes, breach of implied warranty, fraudulent concealment, and breach of privacy laws. The Ninth Circuit upheld the district court's decision. According to the Ninth Circuit:

> The district court was correct in noting that "plaintiffs have not, for example, alleged a demonstrable effect on the market for their specific vehicles based on documented recalls or declining Kelley Bluebook values . . . [n]or have they alleged a risk so immediate that they were forced to replace or discontinue using their vehicles, thus incurring out-of-pocket damages." Additionally, "[n]early 100% of cars on the market include wireless technologies that could pose vulnerabilities to hacking or privacy intrusions." Thus, plaintiffs have only made conclusory allegations that their cars are worth less and have not alleged sufficient facts to establish Article III standing.

Although the result in *Cahen* suggests that an actual attack would have to occur in order for plaintiffs to demonstrate damages, *Flynn v. FCA US LLC* indicates that claims based on potential hacking may be viable even without an actual attack.[27] *Flynn* was a "car hacking" class action filed in 2015. Like the plaintiffs in *Cahen*, the plaintiffs in *Flynn* alleged that hackers could exploit security vulnerabilities and remotely control vehicles. The plaintiffs brought an array of warranty and fraud

---

26 *Cahen v. Toyota Motor Corp.*, 147 F. Supp. 3d 955, N.D. Cal., 2015; *Cahen v. Toyota Motor Corp.*, No. 16-15496, 9th Cir., December 21, 2017.

27 *Flynn v. FCA US LLC*, No. 3: 15-cv 855, S.D. Ill., 2015.

claims on behalf of a putative class of consumers who had purchased Chryslers. The plaintiffs' damages theories were key issues in the case. The plaintiffs' first damages theory was that purchasers reasonably expected and paid for information security when they purchased their vehicles and were entitled to recover the percentage of the sales price that was attributable to information security. The plaintiffs' second damages theory was that their damages could be measured by calculating the costs of repairing security flaws in each car. Although the court rejected the plaintiffs' second damages theory, the court granted in part the plaintiffs' motion for class certification, finding that the overpayment damages theory matched their theory of liability and could be proven on a class-wide basis under the laws of three states. (The court rejected nationwide certification, stating that "it would be unwieldy and require highly individualized inquiries.") In short, a plaintiff can argue that they suffered damages even in the absence of an actual attack, but the differing results in *Cahen* and *Flynn* make it unclear whether this argument would be successful.

### Comparative and Contributory Negligence

In most states, fault for damages caused by hacked AVs (and other scenarios giving rise to negligence claims) may be apportioned among causal actors with legal responsibility under the doctrine of comparative negligence. Fault is apportioned according to the individual's "awareness or indifference with respect to the risks created . . . and any intent with respect to the harm caused . . . and the strength of the causal connection between the person's risk-creating conduct and the harm."[28] For example, a partially autonomous vehicle may provide a lane departure warning (Croft, 2013). If the driver of the partially autonomous vehicle does not take control of the vehicle within a reasonable amount of time, a court may find that driver partially or wholly responsible for the accident (Croft, 2013). Thus, if the AV strikes another vehicle, liability for the crash might be apportioned between the driver and the AV manufacturer.

[28] Restatement (Third) of Torts: Apportionment Liability § 8, 2000.

As of 2016, four states and the District of Columbia use contributory negligence instead of comparative negligence (Di Caro, 2016). *Contributory negligence* refers to conduct undertaken by a plaintiff that created an unreasonable risk to the plaintiff. For example, if an AV owner sues an AV manufacturer after a hacker takes advantage of a vulnerability in software incorporated in the AV's system, the manufacturer could argue that the AV owner was contributorily negligent if the owner rejected an important security update that would have eliminated the vulnerability in the software. If the AV manufacturer is able to prove the contributory negligence claim, the AV owner may be barred from recovering damages or the damages may be reduced.

**Strict Product Liability**

Strict liability is an alternative theory of liability that courts apply in the product liability context when a product is "unreasonably dangerous." An injured party does not have to prove unreasonable conduct under a strict liability theory. Under the Second Restatement and case law that adopts the restatement's strict liability formulation, a manufacturer can be liable for "unreasonably dangerous" defect even if it has "exercised all possible care in the preparation and sale" of the product.[29] Lawsuits arising from conventional automobile design are often brought under a strict product liability theory (Anderson et al., 2016). Anderson et al. (2016) predicts that strict product liability will play a role in lawsuits arising from AV crashes, and Glancy (2015) predicts that the vast majority of states will apply strict liability rather than negligence in lawsuits arising from AV crashes.

Most states recognize three different types of defects for which a defendant may be liable: (1) manufacturing defects, (2) design defects, and (3) warning defects.[30]

***Manufacturing Defects***

Villasenor (2014) provides an example of a manufacturing defect: An AV manufacturer may incorporate well-tested automatic braking soft-

[29] Restatement (Second) of Torts § 402A, 1965.

[30] See Restatement (Third) of Torts: Prods. Liab. § 2.

ware into its vehicles. If the manufacturer accidentally incorporates a flawed prototype version of the software into one of its vehicles and the vehicle crashes because of the software flaw, then the manufacturer could be strictly liable for this manufacturing defect. Similarly, in the AV context, a manufacturer might test sensor software that is not vulnerable to cyberattacks and incorporate the software into its AVs. If the manufacturer accidentally incorporates a flawed version of the software that is vulnerable to cyberattacks, the manufacturer as a result may be found strictly liable for a manufacturing defect.

### *Design Defects*

Many courts use a cost-benefit or risk-utility test to determine whether a design is defective, although the factors considered in this analysis and the standards for conducting it vary from state to state (Anderson et al., 2016; Villasenor, 2014). "[L]itigation about whether a product is unreasonably dangerous often introduces an analysis of the reasonableness of the manufacturer's actions—a study that usually resembles the analysis of reasonableness that occurs in negligence cases" (Anderson et al., 2016). Some states have adopted Section 2 of the American Law Institute's formulation of strict liability, which adopts a reasonableness-based, risk-utility balancing test as the standard for adjudging the defectiveness of product designs and warnings. It also makes clear that even a dangerous product is not defective unless there is proof of a reasonable alternative design.[31] Comments to Section 2 also specify that the risk-benefit balancing done to judge product design must be done

---

[31] For example, in *Flynn et al. v. American Honda Motor Co. Inc.*, No. 4:11-cv-3908, S.D. Tex., 2015, the court found that there was no evidence in support of the plaintiffs' design defect theory because the plaintiffs failed to offer a "safer alternate design." Jacqueline Flynn died when her Honda Civic was struck in a collision. The plaintiffs, Flynn's parents, alleged that there was a delay of critical milliseconds in the deployment of her airbag due to a design defect in the airbag. Under the relevant Texas statute, a "safer alternate design" is a product design that in reasonable probability

> (1) would have prevented or significantly reduced the risk of the plaintiff's personal injury, property damage, or death without substantially impairing the product's utility; and (2) was economically and technologically feasible at the time the product left the control of the manufacturer or seller by the application of existing or reasonably achievable scientific knowledge.

in light of knowledge attainable at the time the product was distributed. The comments also suggest that industry practice and the state of the art are relevant to the balancing analysis. Thus, under a design defect analysis, a court would determine whether the benefits of incorporating alternative technology that would be less vulnerable to cyberattacks outweigh the costs of adopting such technology. If alternative technology would be very costly but would only slightly reduce the risk of an attack that causes only mild damage, then the court would likely find that failure to incorporate the alternative technology does not constitute a design defect.

#### *Warning Defects*

Manufacturers have a duty to warn of hidden dangers in their products. Anderson et al. (2016) notes that "many stakeholders anticipate that cars will be wirelessly connected to the Internet to permit software and other updates to the car's operating systems. In theory, this will allow near instantaneous warnings to be sent by the manufacturers to any category or subcategory of cars relatively easily." The ease of providing warnings might increase a manufacturer's responsibility to monitor and warn against potential vulnerabilities in the AV's systems (Smith, 2013).

As Glancy (2015) notes, proving that the manufacture or design of a product or the failure to warn of a hidden danger made a product "not reasonably safe" will be complicated, given that the AV "blends interactive technologies and components from a number of sources."

### Violation of Consumer Protection Statutes

State consumer protection statutes "vary widely from state to state," but "their basic premise is that unfair and deceptive tactics in the marketplace are inappropriate" (Glancy, 2015). Depending on the scope

---

The plaintiffs' expert offered "only a generalized concept for a design," which consisted of an alternative algorithm to convert data from a car's sensors into a signal that tells the airbags when to deploy. The alternative algorithm had not been tested in any vehicles and "Plaintiffs presented no evidence of either an estimate or a range of the cost of implementing [the] alternative algorithm." Thus, the court found that there was no evidence of a safer alternate design and granted summary judgment in favor of Honda.

of the relevant state statute, AV manufacturers may be sued for violation of consumer protection statutes as a result of cyberattacks on AVs (Glancy, 2015). In the *Cahen* class action discussed above, which arose from risks associated with CANs that connect ECUs in Toyota, Ford, and GM cars, the plaintiffs alleged that Toyota, Ford, and GM concealed material facts concerning the quality, safety, and functionality of vehicles equipped with these systems. The plaintiffs included causes of action for violation of various state consumer protection laws based on these alleged misrepresentations as well as misleading advertising. However, as noted above, the *Cahen* class action was not successful because the plaintiffs had not suffered any actual damages. Even in the presence of actual damages, the likelihood of success on a cause of action anchored in a state consumer protection statute will vary from state to state because the scope and effectiveness of these laws is different in each state, with some state laws "[p]rohibiting only a few narrow types of unfairness and deception" and some applying only to a "few businesses" (Carter, 2009).

### Misrepresentation, Fraud, and Fraudulent Concealment

Generally, defendants can be held liable for misrepresentation if they make a false or misleading statement and a plaintiff suffers harm as a result of reasonably relying on the statement. Plaintiffs might bring misrepresentation or fraud claims if AV manufacturers conceal material facts about vulnerabilities in their systems. An issue that has arisen in products liability contexts and that is likely to arise in the context of AVs is whether the manufacturer of a system that integrates another company's software may be liable for concealing problems with the software. As noted above, in the lawsuits arising out of the American Airlines Flight 965 crash, which was caused in part by the poor design of the navigational database programmed into the flight management computer, the plaintiffs brought causes of action for intentional misrepresentation, negligent misrepresentation, and fraudulent concealment against Honeywell, Inc. (the supplier of the aircraft's flight management computer), and Jeppesen Sanderson, Inc. (which provided the navigational database programmed into the flight management computer and the corresponding aviation charts).[32] In the context of AVs, which blend software, parts, and systems from a variety of sources, the issue of which parties had knowledge of vulnerabilities in parts and systems that they incorporated into their products will likely arise under fraud and misrepresentation claims.

### Warranty Theories

The theories of liability discussed above are based in product liability law. Warranty liability based in contract law may also be relevant if a defect makes an AV susceptible to cyberattack resulting in damage to the purchaser of the AV. Although, in general, product liability does not allow for recovery of purely economic losses, warranty law provides a basis for recovery of economic losses. Under the UCC's implied warranty of merchantability, by placing a product such as an AV into the stream of commerce, manufacturers and sellers impliedly certify that the product is reasonably capable of its intended use. In the *Cahen* class action discussed above, the plaintiffs alleged that CANs that connected ECUs in Toyota, Ford, and GM vehicles were vulnerable to attacks that would allow hackers to gain control of AVs' braking, steering, and acceleration. The plaintiffs brought causes of action against Toyota and GM for breach of California's, Oregon's, and Washington's implied warranty of merchantability, based on the allegation that the "vehicles were not in merchantable condition and were not fit for the ordinary purpose for which cars are used because of the defects in the CAN buses."[33]

However, alleging and proving economic loss under breach of warranty claims may be difficult in the absence of an actual attack. As noted in the negligence discussion above, a plaintiff can argue that they suffered damages even in the absence of an actual attack, but the differing results in *Cahen* and *Flynn* make it unclear whether this argument would be successful.

---

[32] *Tafuri v. Jeppesen Sanderson, Inc.*, 25 F. Supp. 2d 1364, Dist. Court, S.D. Fla., 1998.

[33] *Helene Cahen et al. v. Toyota Motor Corporation et al.*, case no. 3:15-cv-01104, U.S. District Court for the Northern District of California, First Amended Complaint.

In addition, even if an attack occurs, a buyer's damages for breach of warranty will typically be limited to the "difference at the time and place of acceptance between the value of the goods accepted and the value they would have had if they had been as warranted."[34]

State and federal "lemon laws," which require repair or replacement of defective products, will also be relevant if product defects make AVs vulnerable to cyberattacks. Lemon law programs have been used to require repair or replacement of traditional automobiles and would apply to AVs as well.[35]

### Privacy Laws

Use of AVs will involve the collection, storage, and use of a wide variety of personal information.[36] Glancy (2012) notes that AVs will generate information on where trips start and end, location information, and other types of personal data and predicts that entities interested in personal information generated by AVs will include advertisers, law enforcement, and intelligence agencies. Kohler and Colbert-Taylor (2014) notes,

> Although exclusively sensor-based autonomous vehicles are certainly a possibility, many of the most compelling reasons for adopting self-driving cars are dependent on the vehicles sharing and coordinating data with each other, both locally and through centralized infrastructure. It is self-evident that the efficient management of traffic at intersections, the intelligent distribution of

---

[34] See Uniform Commercial Code § 2-714(2).

[35] See, e.g., Magnuson-Moss Warranty Act, 15 U.S.C. §§ 2301–2312, 2012; International Association of Lemon Law Administrators, 2018 (providing information about state Lemon Law statutes).

[36] Although state and federal government use of personal information generated by AVs is not within the scope of this report, is worth noting that the Drivers' Privacy Protection Act (which applies to personal information processed by state DMVs), 49 U.S.C. § 30111(a) (establishing requirements for NHTSA to follow when issuing motor vehicle safety standards), the Constitutional Bill of Rights (which protects against government intrusion), and the Privacy Act of 1974, H.R. Rep. No. 89-1919, at 2732 (1966), would apply. For a discussion of laws and regulations that would apply if government entities access information produced and used by AVs, see Glancy (2012).

> traffic to minimize congestion, and the ability of autonomous vehicles to safely travel in close-packed platoons, for instance, are all largely or completely reliant on communication both between the individual vehicles and other cars in the vicinity, and between the autonomous vehicles and an external network.

Notably, recent enactments provide monetary damages for breaches of personal information—including geolocation information—even in the absence of actual harm to consumers. The California Consumer Privacy Act, AB 375 (2017–2018, effective date January 1, 2020), provides consumers with a private right of action against businesses that fail to "implement and maintain reasonable security procedures and practices appropriate to the nature of the information to protect the personal information," resulting in "unauthorized access and exfiltration, theft, or disclosure" of "nonencrypted or nonredacted personal information." The act specifically includes geolocation data under the definition of personal information and "does not expressly condition liability on this data being misused in a way that harms consumers" (Lilley, Weinberg, and Parasharami, 2018). The European Union's General Data Protection Regulation (GDPR), which took effect on May 25, 2018, also imposes fines against companies whose failure to protect personal data results in data breaches, and the GDPR defines personal data to include location data (European Union GDPR Portal, undated). In addition, a recent U.S. Supreme Court ruling makes it more likely that geolocation information collected by AV-involved entities will be considered highly sensitive in privacy litigation. In its June 2018 decision in *Carpenter v. U.S.*,[37] the U.S. Supreme Court held that government actors must obtain a warrant to acquire detailed, long-term geolocation information collected from mobile phones by cellular towers. The data collection at issue—comprehensive long-term collection of an individual's past locations—is the type of personal information that would likely be collected by AVs. Even though the holding only directly applies to government actors in the Fourth Amendment "search and seizure" context, the plaintiffs' lawyers have indicated

---

[37] *Carpenter v. US*, 585 U. S. ____, 2018.

their intention to cite the case in support of arguments in data security litigation that location information is highly sensitive (Ropes & Gray, 2018). In addition, if locational and other private information is breached, the parties who generate, collect, and/or use the information may face liability under the privacy breach statutes that have been enacted in 47 states (Glancy, 2012). These laws generally require that if information is improperly disclosed through data breaches, the party who collected the personal information (e.g., AV manufacturers, AV sellers, ride-service companies) must notify these individuals (Glancy, 2012). Providing the notification required under these statutes involves significant monetary and reputational costs (Glancy, 2012).

## Damages Available Under Tort Theories

Under traditional tort law, successful plaintiffs are entitled to recover compensatory damages intended to compensate them for harm suffered. These damages may include economic damages to compensate the plaintiff for monetary loss, such as the payment of medical expenses. Plaintiffs also sometimes recover noneconomic damages, such as for pain and suffering. If a defendant's behavior is particularly bad, a plaintiff may also recover punitive damages, which are intended to deter the defendant and others from similar conduct in the future.

Car manufacturers have been held liable for punitive damages when they knew of a danger and failed to remedy it.[38] As discussed above, in *General Motors Corp. v. Johnston*, a Chevrolet pickup truck stalled in an intersection and was struck by a logging truck, killing the passenger in the Chevrolet pickup truck. GM was aware of the stalling problem in its pickup trucks but did not take remedial action to protect drivers of the trucks.[39] In this case, the court awarded $15 million in punitive damages.[40]

---

[38] See, e.g., *General Motors Corp. v. Johnston*, 1992; *Am. Motors Corp. v. Ellis*, 403 So. 2d 459, 468, Fla. Dist. Ct. App., 1981.

[39] *General Motors Corp. v. Johnston*, 1992.

[40] *General Motors Corp. v. Johnston*, 1992.

## Summarizing Liability Theories in the Context of Hacked Autonomous Vehicles

Parties such as AV manufacturers, manufacturers and designers of component parts and software, and distributors of AVs may face civil liability for criminal hacks of AVs. Drivers of AVs may also face liability for cyberattacks if, for example, they reject an important security update that allows a hacker to take control of the AV and steer it into another vehicle. Because there are very few federal and state laws on autonomous and connected vehicles, product liability laws—along with warranty law and state and federal privacy laws—are likely to be the most relevant body of law in lawsuits arising specifically from cyberattacks on AVs.

Negligence and strict liability are two legal theories that are likely to play critical roles in civil lawsuits arising from cyberattacks on AVs. Both of these theories involve balancing the foreseeability of specific cyberattacks and costs associated with adopting alternate technologies that are less vulnerable to hacks. Because an understanding of risks associated with AVs and technology that may protect against cyberattacks is necessary in this balancing analysis, technical knowledge of courts and evolving industry knowledge and standards will play a significant role in lawsuits arising from cyberattacks.

In the next chapter, we introduce hypothetical scenarios of cyberattacks on AVs and use the legal framework detailed in this chapter to analyze legal liability issues that arise under each scenario.

CHAPTER SEVEN

# Legal Analysis of Hypothetical Risk Scenarios

This chapter marries an analysis of existing theories of civil liability to four scenarios to help decisionmakers and other interested parties understand via illustration where policy responses may be useful. As mentioned in the introduction, elements of the scenarios are based on real-world examples to make them more plausible.

## Scenario 1: Ransomware

A lone-wolf hacker has figured out a way to send malware via Bluetooth to an AV remotely by exploiting a vulnerability in the AV's entertainment system. Joe Smith, the car's owner, is unaware of the vulnerability. The malware successfully gains access to the CAN of the AV, putting the hacker in a position to exchange data and instructions with other ECUs connected to the CAN. Once activated, the malware uses the AV's built-in cellular internet connectivity (provided by AT&T) to connect to the attacker's command and control network.

The hacker then sends an instruction to kill the engine and employs a similar technique to disable the onboard diagnostics port and over-the-air upgrade mechanism—effectively fencing out anyone who might intervene. Once the engine is killed, the attacker disables the cylinders (to prevent the engine from starting up) and also disables steering and brakes. The hacker also locks the AV's doors by continuously activating the lock relay, denying physical access to the car.

The attacker sends a message to Joe Smith demanding payment of $5,000 via untraceable cryptocurrency within 12 hours on the threat of driving the AV into a wall. The owner calls law enforcement, his mechanic, and the manufacturer, none of whom can help him in time. The driver does not pay, and the attacker drives the car into a wall, damaging it severely.

The authorities are unable to identify the hacker, leaving Joe Smith few options but to seek recompense through the civil justice system.

He sues the car company for the vulnerabilities it was directly responsible for (e.g., the car's operating system) as well as the components it sold or integrated (e.g., Bluetooth, engine). His suit also alleges that the manufacturer falsely represented that in the event that the car's normal operations were disrupted, the car company could restore the car's normal operations via over-the-air upgrades. (However, the hacker disabled the over-the-air capabilities, preventing the company from restoring the car's normal operations.) Joe Smith also sues the cellular company, AT&T, for not preventing the hacker from using its internet connectivity to transmit his instructions. He sues the company that manufactured the car's engine for the underlying vulnerabilities that allowed the hacker access to the CAN and ECUs.

Joes sues for the sticker price of his car.

During discovery, the Bluetooth component manufacturer discovers that its software development system was breached by some unknown third party, allowing Joe Smith's hacker to install the malware. Neither the identity of Joe Smith's hacker, nor that of the attacker that breached the Bluetooth manufacturer's system, is ever determined. Nevertheless, Joe adds the Bluetooth manufacturer as a defendant.

In a lawsuit that arose from this scenario, Joe Smith would likely bring causes of action for negligence, strict liability, fraud/misrepresentation, and breach of warranty.

### Negligence

The plaintiff in this scenario filed suit against the car manufacturer, the component part manufacturers, and the internet service provider. As detailed in Chapter Six, a plaintiff would have to prove duty, breach, causation, and damages to bring a lawsuit against these defendants under a negligence cause of action. For breach of duty, courts in product liability lawsuits commonly have used a cost-benefit analysis. In order to prove breach of duty, the plaintiff would have to identify a precaution that each defendant could have taken or superior technology that each defendant could have adopted to prevent the attack.

For example, the plaintiff would have to identify (1) an alternative to CAN technology or more-secure CAN technology that the AV manufacturer could have adopted, (2) the technology and/or process that the cell phone company could have adopted to prevent its network from being used to launch the cyberattack, and (3) an alternative to the ECUs or more-secure ECUs that the engine company could have adopted. The plaintiff would also have to prove that the costs to each defendant of adopting the precautionary measures are outweighed by the risks involved with not taking the measure (i.e., damage to the AV resulting from the hack).

As detailed in the previous chapter, federal and state laws relating to AVs are still being developed. As federal and state laws are enacted, courts will likely take relevant laws into account in making civil liability determinations. Joe could offer evidence of breach of a relevant law to demonstrate that a defendant breached their duty. If there are no federal or state laws relevant to this scenario, Joe could offer evidence of industry customs to demonstrate breach of the duty. Owen (2004) lists cases in which a court admitted evidence of a manufacturer's failure to comply with industry standards as proof of the manufacturer's negligence. Products at issue in these cases include (1) a tire that was not equipped with technology to prevent belt separation that was known and generally used in the tire industry;[1] (2) machinery and equipment that was not equipped with an emergency stop device, as required under an American Society of Mechanical Engineers standard;[2] and (3) brakes that did not comply with Society of Automotive Engineers standards.[3] However, unlike relevant statutes (the violation of which

---

1 *Morden v. Cont. AG*, 611 N.W.2d 659, 675–676, Wis., 2000.

2 *Almazan v. CTB, Inc.*, No. CIV.A.SA-99-CA355PMA, 2000 WL 33348244, at *10, W.D. Tex., April 27, 2000.

3 See *Hasson v. Ford Motor Co.*, 650 P.2d 1171, 1182–1183, Cal., 1982.

can establish prima facie breach of duty), industry standards are not legally binding.

In making a causation determination, the court might consider whether the defendants may be held liable for damages resulting from the cyberattack. As noted in Chapter Six, although criminal actions by a third party may cut off liability for a manufacturing or design flaw, proximate cause may be preserved if the defendant's wrongdoing created a tempting opportunity for parties who would not be deterred by threat of a judgment. Here, the security vulnerabilities in the CAN and the ECUs and the cell phone company's failure to choke off access by the attacker lowered the hacker's transaction costs by making the attack faster and more efficient, remotely executable, and less likely to be blocked. Because foreseeability will play a critical role in the encouragement of bad actors analysis, evidence of prior instances of hackers taking advantage of the same or similar vulnerabilities would be persuasive to the court.

In addition, with respect to causation, as noted in the previous chapter, most courts adopt the "but for" test to establish cause-in-fact. Here, it appears that the plaintiff would be able to establish cause-in-fact with respect to each defendant because without the vulnerability in each component or system, the attack would not have occurred. An example of the "but for" test failing would be if the plaintiff alleged that the car company negligently failed to activate the upgrade in his car, but the upgrade would not have prevented the attack to begin with. Proximate causation, as noted previously, requires that a defendant's conduct be "reasonably related" to the plaintiff's harm in order for the defendant to be liable. To be "reasonably related" to a plaintiff's harm, a defendant's conduct must be within the scope of reasonably foreseeable injury (de Villiers, 2004). As noted, with respect to crashes that result solely from defective technology (i.e., when no third-party bad actor is involved), crashes are generally a reasonably foreseeable consequence of defective automated technology (Wittenberg, 2016). However, when a third-party bad actor is involved, the issue of foreseeability is more complex. In the context of cyberattacks on AVs, the central question will be whether the injury caused by a third-party bad actor was a foreseeable result of the defendant manufacturer's or AV owner's negligence. Whether the chain of events was foreseeable in this case will again depend in large part on whether similar attacks by third-party bad actors have occurred so that each defendant could have foreseen that failure to take the precaution at issue would lead to an attack.

The damages element of a negligence cause of action will likely be easy to prove in this case because there was physical damage to the car.

### Strict Liability

If a court determines that manufacturing defects, design defects, or warning defects in the AV rendered the vehicle "unreasonably dangerous," the plaintiff would not have to prove unreasonable conduct. However, in making a strict liability determination, a court would likely still perform a cost-benefit analysis and consider industry standards. Thus, to be successful on a strict liability claim, the plaintiff would have to demonstrate that the benefits of an alternative design or warning outweigh costs, as detailed in the negligence analysis above.

### Misrepresentation, Fraud, and Fraudulent Concealment

A defendant can be held liable for misrepresentation if they make a false or misleading statement and a plaintiff suffers harm as a result of reasonably relying on the statement. Here, Joe Smith alleges that the car company misrepresented that the car's over-the-air upgrade capability would work, thus preventing this kind of attack. If a plaintiff reasonably relied on this misrepresentation and his reliance on the misrepresentation led to the harm he suffered, he could be successful on a misrepresentation claim. However, if he still would have purchased the car absent the upgrade capability and/or would not have taken any extra precautions even in the absence of the upgrade capability, then he might not be able to argue that he relied on a misrepresentation to his detriment.

Another issue that may arise relevant to this cause of action is whether the AV manufacturer may be liable for concealing problems with the parts and systems that are incorporated into its vehicle. In other words, a court might consider the AV manufacturer liable for vulnerabilities in the component parts (Bluetooth and engine) if the manufacturer were aware of vulnerabilities and concealed those vulnerabilities.

### Violation of Consumer Protection Statutes

As noted in Chapter Six, state consumer protection statutes' "basic premise is that unfair and deceptive tactics in the marketplace are inappropriate" (Carter, 2009). In this case, the potential liability of the defendants would depend on the law of the state in which Joe Smith sued. The *Cahen* class action detailed in Chapter Six arose from risks associated with CANs that connect ECUs in Toyota, Ford, and GM cars. Plaintiffs in the Toyota class action alleged that defendant vehicle manufacturers concealed material facts concerning the quality, safety, and functionality of vehicles equipped with CANs. The plaintiffs included causes of action for violation of various state consumer protection laws based on these alleged misrepresentations and misleading advertising. In this case, the plaintiff could bring similar claims against the AV manufacturer and the manufacturers and designers of the component parts and systems. However, as noted above, the requirements, scope, and effectiveness of these statutes varies widely from state to state, so the success of the claim would depend on the relevant state statute. Under most state unfair and deceptive practices statutes, Joe would have to prove (1) that the defendants engaged in conduct that caused him or other consumers substantial injury, (2) that the injury could not be reasonably avoided, and (3) that the potential harm was not outweighed by countervailing benefits to consumers. The first two of these elements would be relatively easy to prove, but the court would have to engage in a balancing analysis with respect to the third element (Carter, 2009).

### Warranty Law

The car manufacturer and the component part manufacturers may be found liable under warranty theories in Joe Smith's case. In the *Cahen* class action, the plaintiffs also brought claims for breach of implied warranty based on the allegation that the vehicles were not in merchantable condition and were not fit for the ordinary purpose for which cars are used because of the defects in the CAN buses.[4] However, as noted above, in the absence of an actual attack, the *Cahen* plaintiffs were unsuccessful.[5] In this scenario, because an actual attack occurred, the plaintiff would have a higher likelihood of success on a warranty claim. However, as noted in Chapter Six, damages would likely be limited to the difference "between the value of the goods accepted and the value they would have had if they had been as warranted."[6]

As emphasized by the *Cahen* case, damages will likely be a threshold issue in lawsuits involving attacks and potential attacks on AVs. In scenarios such as Scenario 1, in which damages are easy to prove, major issues will likely be whether the attack was foreseeable and whether the benefits of avoiding the attack outweigh the costs of the attack. In making the foreseeability determination, courts will likely consider technology and industry standards and customs relating to the technology. In order to prevail, component part manufacturers and vehicle manufacturers would need to ensure that their products not only comply with federal, state, and local law but also comply with evolving industry standards. The issue of foreseeability will also turn on whether similar attacks have occurred in the past. Manufacturers of vehicles and component parts would need to stay abreast of attacks on AVs and take any necessary precautions to avoid similar attacks if they wish to avoid lawsuits. In addition, plaintiffs and defendants who find themselves in lawsuits such as this one will likely need to hire experts to assist the court in identifying alternative technologies and determining whether the costs of adopting alternative technology that is less vulnerable to attacks or other precautionary measures are outweighed by risks involved with not taking the measure.

---

4 *Helene Cahen et al. v. Toyota Motor Corporation et al.*, First Amended Complaint.

5 *Helene Cahen et al. v. Toyota Motor Corporation et al.*, First Amended Complaint.

6 See Uniform Commercial Code § 2-714(2).

## Scenario 2: Military Base Damage

Maria Cruz, a lieutenant assigned to Lemoore Air Force Base in California's Central Valley, drives an AV to work.[7] One day, the car drives Cruz onto the base, parks in its assigned spot, and Cruz goes into her office. While she's working, an unidentified hacker gains access to the car by activating previously installed malware that was installed via the car's over-the-air update functionality. The hacker takes control of the AV's ignition, starting the car. The attacker then disengages the brakes, applies the accelerator, and steers the vehicle remotely, targeting a nearby airstrip.

Cruz's AV careens down a runway toward an FA-18E fighter jet parked by a hangar. Accelerating to 60 mph, the AV crashes into the jet, damaging its horizontal stabilizer and other components. The cost of repairing the jet totals $60 million.

The U.S. government sues the car's manufacturer, the component part manufacturers, and the owner of the vehicle to recover those costs.

### Government as Plaintiff in a Suit for Negligent Damage to Government Property

As AVs enter the public sphere, AV crashes are likely to affect government property, be it street signs, roadways, bridges, or military bases. Whether these crashes will give rise to legal claims by the government will depend on what type of recovery the government seeks. As Prosser and Keeton (1984) stated, "The state never can sue in tort in its political or governmental capacity, although as the owner of property it may resort to the same tort actions as any individual proprietor to recover for injuries to the property, or to recover the property itself."

In practical terms, this means that if a party's negligence causes a crash that damages government property, the government may recover damages for harm to the property, but not for any rescue and cleanup efforts it undertook as a result of the crash (Krauss, 2007). For example, in *District of Columbia v Air Florida, Inc.*, the District of Columbia

---

[7] This scenario was informed by a real-world incident that did not involve AVs but resulted in damage similar to that described here (Doyle, 2016).

sued an airline after a jet crashed into a bridge in the district during takeoff.[8] The district sued for damages to the bridge and also sought to recover for its expenditures on emergency services for jet passengers and bridge motorists.[9] The airline agreed to pay damages to the district for damage to the bridge, but the court dismissed the claims against the airline for the costs of rescue services.[10] The court found that the airline had no duty to not prompt use of the district fire department's emergency services.[11] Other courts also rejected government attempts to recover costs of public services from a negligent tortfeasor, finding that no preexisting duty existed to the government to refrain from prompting the use of their emergency services (Krauss, 2007). In this scenario, the government sued the car's manufacturer, the component part manufacturers, and the owner of the vehicle. If the court were to find that any of the defendants were negligent, the government would likely be able to recover for damages to the airplane. However, if anyone had been injured during the crash, the government would be unlikely to recover for expenses incurred in any rescue efforts because the court would likely find that no preexisting duty existed to refrain from prompting the use of government emergency services.

The government might be successful on negligence and strict liability claims against the AV manufacturer, as well as component part and system manufacturers. Several other claims are unlikely to apply because they apply only between sellers and purchasers, and, in this case, the government, as the plaintiff, is not the owner of the car. These other claims include unfair trade practices, misrepresentations about the AV's safety or capabilities, and warranty liability.

## Negligence

With respect to the negligence claims, damages will be the easiest element to prove because the cyberattack resulted in $60 million in dam-

---

8 *District of Columbia v. Air Florida, Inc.*, 750 F.2d, 1077–1078, D.C. Cir., 1984.

9 *District of Columbia v. Air Florida, Inc.*, 1984.

10 *District of Columbia v. Air Florida, Inc.*, 1984, p. 1080.

11 *District of Columbia v. Air Florida, Inc.*, 1984, p. 1080.

ages. Breach of duty will involve an analysis similar to the analysis outlined under Scenario 1. For example, the government would likely have to identify alternatives to the compromised AV parts and systems that the manufacturer could have adopted. The government would also likely have to demonstrate that the costs of adopting such alternate technology were outweighed by the risks involved in not adopting it. The government could also offer evidence of a breach of a relevant cybersecurity standard to demonstrate that a defendant breached their duty or offer evidence of informal industry customs to demonstrate breach of the duty.

The causation determination will also involve an analysis similar to the analysis outlined under Scenario 1. Was the cyberattack foreseeable so that the encouragement of free radical paradigm might apply, and has proximate causation been shown? As under Scenario 1, whether the chain of events was foreseeable depends in large part on whether similar attacks have occurred so that each defendant could have foreseen that failure to take the precaution at issue would lead to an attack. In making the foreseeability determination, the court will also likely consider technology and industry standards and customs relating to the technology.

Contributory negligence might also be an issue in this case. As noted in Chapter Six, *contributory negligence* refers to conduct undertaken by a plaintiff that created an unreasonable risk to the plaintiff. Here, defendants might argue that the government was contributorily negligent in allowing an AV onto the military base. If AVs have been hacked outside of a laboratory setting, then the defendants would have a stronger argument that the government knowingly exposed itself to a risk and was therefore contributorily negligent.

### Strict Liability

As detailed in Chapter Six, courts apply strict product liability when a product is "unreasonably dangerous." An injured party does not have to prove unreasonable conduct under a strict liability theory. Strict liability claims are applicable to AV users and injured parties even if they did not purchase the product at issue. Thus, the government could bring a strict product liability claim against the manufacturer of the

AV and the component part manufacturers. As under Scenario 1, the court's strict liability analysis will likely involve a cost-benefit analysis and consideration of industry standards at the time.

## Scenario 3: Hacking of Infrastructure

An attacker hacks into the infrastructure for controlling traffic and gains unauthorized access to wirelessly networked traffic lights. The attacker then maliciously manipulates the traffic lights at a busy junction on a state highway such that two roads that are perpendicular to each other are given a green light simultaneously. A city-owned autonomous bus carrying a few passengers is traveling at a high speed down one road. It correctly identifies the green light and continues to drive straight ahead and does not halt when a car from the perpendicular road drives in front of it. The bus crashes into the car, causing severe damage to the car.

In this scenario, the potential plaintiff car driver might allege that the state department of transportation is liable for the crash because of the vulnerability in the traffic light. A potential plaintiff might also argue that the city is liable for the crash because a city-owned autonomous bus should have recognized that lights were green in all directions at the intersection and stopped accordingly. In addition, the plaintiff might bring a lawsuit against the manufacturer of the software integrated into the public bus and the manufacturer of the bus who incorporated the software into the design of the bus.

In a potential lawsuit against the state department of transportation or the city's transit authority, a threshold issue would be whether sovereign immunity would shield the city from liability. Historically, state and federal governments and their agents were immune from civil liability under the doctrine of sovereign immunity.[12] However, the federal government abandoned the sovereign immunity doctrine in 1945

---

[12] See *Ngiraingas v. Sanchez*, 495 U.S. 182, 203, 1998 (J. Brennan, dissenting); *Kawananakoa v. Polyblank*, 205 U.S. 349, 353–354, 1907.

via the Federal Tort Claims Act (FTCA),[13] and most states have also enacted statutes similar to the FTCA.[14]

An exception to the FTCA and similar state law exceptions eliminate a government's responsibility for the "discretionary" functions of its employees, as opposed to those that are purely "ministerial."[15] In general, discretionary functions include activities that involve significant public policy decisionmaking.[16] Thus, if a court considered ensuring the security of traffic light systems discretionary, the state department of transportation would be immune from suit, but if the court considered this function ministerial, the state department of transportation would not be immune from suit.

In considering potential lawsuits against government agencies in the context of AVs, Boeglin (2015) concludes that the sovereign immunity doctrine would shield governments from liability in intelligent highway scenarios: "Sovereign immunity, which immunizes the state against civil and/or criminal suits, has often been invoked to negate suits for accidents that occur on public transit systems or as a result of regulatory decision-making." Glancy (2015) also considers the issue

---

[13] 28 U.S.C. § 1346.

[14] Calnan and Taslitz, 1999, p. 177, citing Alaska Stat. § 18.80.200 (Michie, 1998); Cal. Civ. Code § 51.7 (West, 1982, and Supp., 2000); Conn. Gen. Stat. § 46a-58, 1983; Idaho Code § 18-7301, 1997; Ind. Code Ann. §§ 22-9-1-1 to -18 (Michie, 1997, and Supp., 1999); Iowa Code Ann. § 729.1 (West, 1993, and Supp., 1999); Ky. Rev. Stat. Ann. § 344.010 (Michie, 1997); Me. Rev. Stat. Ann. Tit. 17, § 1301-A (West, 1983, and Supp., 1999); Mich. Comp. Laws Ann. § 750.146 (West, 1991); Minn. Stat. Ann. § 363.03 (West, 1991, and Supp., 2000); Mont. Code Ann. § 49-2-308 (1991 and Supp., 1999); Neb. Rev. Stat. §§ 20-301 to -344 (1997); N.J. Stat. Ann. § 10:1-1 (West, 1993); N.M. Stat. Ann. §§ 28-1-1 to -15 (Michie, 1996); Ohio Rev. Code Ann. § 4112.02 (Anderson, 1998); Or. Rev. Stat. § 30.670 (1997); Wash. Rev. Code Ann. § 9.91.010 (West, 1998); Wis. Stat. Ann. § 106.04 (West, 1997, and Supp., 1999); Wyo. Stat. Ann. § 6-9-102 (Michie, 1999).

[15] 28 U.S.C. § 2680(a).

[16] Ondrovic, 1983, citing *Forsyth v. Eli Lilly & Co.*, 904 F. Supp. 1153, 1159, D. Haw., 1995 (FDA approval of drug); *Laurence v. United States*, 851 F. Supp. 1445, 1450, N.D. Cal., 1994 (government construction for emergency housing during wartime); *Lewis v. United States Navy*, 865 F. Supp. 294, 299, D.S.C., 1994 (disclosure of health effects of gas exposure during World War II); *Evangelical United Brethren Church v. State*, 407 P.2d 440, 445, Wash., 1966 (correction of delinquent children); see also Restatement (Second) of Torts § 895B cmt. d, 1979.

of sovereign immunity in the AV context but concludes that immunity from liability will turn on whether the court considers the government conduct at issue to be ministerial or discretionary: "A third category of potential defendants in civil lawsuits arising out of first-generation autonomous cars would be "peripheral" defendants, such as local governments that fail to repair unsafe roads. The initial design of roads and of potential vehicle communications systems to accommodate first-generation AVs will probably require exercise of significant discretion by the responsible government agencies. However, once the roadway and communications infrastructure is established, its upkeep may provide a ministerial duty basis for civil liability, unprotected by sovereign immunity, on the part of state and local government entities.

Under this reasoning, as AVs and supporting infrastructure develop, government agencies will be more likely to be held civilly liable if their negligence provides the attacker an opportunity to cause a crash. In our scenario, a finding that the state department of transportation or the city's transit authority is liable for the crash will be more likely as time goes on and AVs and their supporting infrastructure develop.

With respect to a lawsuit against the state department of transportation because of the vulnerability in the traffic light, it is worth noting that at least one state department of transportation has been held liable for negligence when a traffic light provided green signals in all directions at an intersection. In this lawsuit against the Virginia Department of Transportation, the plaintiffs crashed into another vehicle at an intersection, causing injuries and damages to the vehicle. Both drivers testified that they had green lights, and the court found the Department of Transportation negligent for improperly maintaining the traffic light.[17]

Our Scenario 3 may be distinguished from the Virginia Department of Transportation case because a hacker, not a technical malfunction, caused the lights to be green in all directions. Thus, a key issue in our case would be whether a plaintiff could recover for inju-

---

[17] *A76-369 SU/Suffolk*, summary available at Virginia Transportation Research Council (2004).

ries arising from a criminal attack on public transportation. The body of law that addresses municipal tort liability for traditional criminal attacks against passengers on mass transportation is instructive on this issue. Ondrovic (1983) notes that there are three primary theories of recovery that allow for municipal liability for injuries arising from criminal attacks on public transportation. The first two are relevant in the AV context. First, when addressing the issue of criminal attacks on public transportation, numerous courts have classified city-run public transportation systems as common carriers, which are held to the highest degree of care and diligence in order to provide passenger safety (Ondrovic, 1983). Although a court's adoption of the common-carrier classification would not guarantee that the city would be found negligent, the higher standard of care would make this finding more likely. The second theory of recovery that Ondrovic (1983) discusses is municipal notice of a dangerous condition. In the context of traditional public transportation, a court might find that prior criminal attacks in an area put the transit authority on notice of the need for police or other protection in that area. In the AV context, if similar attacks have occurred on other traffic light systems, a court would be more likely to find that the attack was foreseeable and, thus, that the city was negligent in failing to prevent the attack (Ondrovic, 1983).

With respect to a lawsuit against the state department of transportation because of the vulnerability in the traffic light, safety standards for government vehicles would likely be relevant to negligence determinations. As noted in Chapter Six, violation of safety guidelines and industry standards can provide evidence of a breach of duty in a negligence analysis. In the future, it is likely that government agencies will promulgate safety standards with respect to AVs. The U.S. Department of Homeland Security Science and Technology Directorate (DHS S&T), the Cyber Security Division, the U.S. Department of Transportation Volpe Center (DOT Volpe), and the nonprofit research institute SRI International formed a Government Vehicle Cybersecurity Steering Group that met in October 2015. The group was assessing potential threats to government vehicles and developing security measures (Davis, 2015). The three primary focus areas of the steering committee are (1) "address[ing] cybersecurity needs for government vehicles," (2) "promot[ing] automotive cybersecurity best practices and guidelines in the private sector," and (3) "discuss[ing] key challenges and develop[ing a] pre-competitive research consortium with industry" (SRI International, 2015). DHS S&T and DOT Volpe released a primer on vehicle telematics in 2018. The primer is a response to Executive Order (EO) 13693 ("Planning for Federal Sustainability in the Next Decade"), issued in 2015, which requires all federal fleet managers to implement telematics systems for their vehicles. (Vehicle telematics are systems embedded in the vehicle that collect information on the vehicle and combine wireless and internet communications to send, receive, and store vehicle information.) DHS S&T and DOT Volpe recognized that, as use of telematics grows, cybersecurity vulnerabilities will increase, necessitating safeguards for the telematics systems. Thus, in response to EO 13693, DHS S&T and DOT Volpe collaborated to create a cybersecurity implementation and operational primer for government fleet managers (DHS, 2018).

A court would likely weigh violation of the best practices and guidelines that the Steering Group and other relevant organizations will develop in a determination of whether the relevant government actor was in fact negligent. For example, in our scenario, if the Steering Group's guidelines recommended that municipal buses be equipped with safety features to prevent crashes in instances where hackers interfere with traffic signals, violation of this recommendation by the municipality would weigh in favor of municipal liability.

With respect to liability against the software manufacturer and the bus manufacturer that integrated the vulnerable software, the analysis would be similar to the analysis under Scenario 1. Potential causes of action arising from the vulnerable software would include negligence and strict liability. Key issues under these causes of action would likely include current industry standards and whether less-vulnerable software could have feasibly been developed and incorporated. If it appears that the software manufacturer and/or the bus manufacturer were aware of software vulnerabilities, a plaintiff would likely also bring causes of action for fraudulent concealment and violation of the relevant state consumer protection law.

## Scenario 4: Theft of Corporate Information

A hacker plants malware in an AV owned by a car rental company, and the malware spreads to the rest of the fleet via the company's computer systems, including reservations and accounting. The malware allows the hacker to access customers' credit card information, which the hacker uses to make fraudulent financial transactions. An advertising company executive who frequents hacker bulletin boards on the dark web reads posts about the rental car company's vulnerability. Using a computer at the advertising agency, he makes use of the vulnerability to obtain location information about the rental car company's clients. The advertising company then uses the location information for geo-targeted advertising. Rental car company clients whose personal information was stolen file a lawsuit against the rental car company for not safeguarding their data.[18]

As noted in the "Privacy Laws" section of Chapter Six, recent enactments such as the California Consumer Privacy Act and the GDPR provide monetary damages for breach of personal information (including geolocation information) even in the absence of harm to consumers. Under the California Consumer Privacy Act, for example, a company can be liable for breach of private data even in the absence of harm resulting from misuse of the data. Under the California Consumer Privacy Act, the rental car company's California clients could bring suit and obtain statutory damages of between $100 and $750

[18] As noted in the beginning of this chapter, this report focuses on civil liability issues that manufacturers of AVs and component parts will face after a cyberattack. In this scenario, the advertising company that stole the location information might face criminal penalties under federal statutes, such the Electronic Communications Privacy Act, 18 U.S.C. §§ 2510–2511 (2012). The advertising agency might also face civil liability under intentional tort theories, such as trespass to chattels or intentional infliction of emotional distress. However, the advertising agency, like other hackers, may be more difficult to identify and bring to court, and thus a plaintiff would likely go after the more easily identifiable target with deeper pockets: the rental car company.

In a scenario like this, a plaintiff might also sue the vehicle manufacturer and component part manufacturers. Potential causes of action would be negligence, strict product liability, and warranty law. The analyses that a court would undertake under each of these causes of action would likely be the same analyses outlined under the negligence, strict product liability, and warranty law causes of action in Scenario 1.

"per consumer per incident or actual damages"[19] and other remedies a court deems appropriate. In fact, the car rental company could face a class action under the California Consumer Privacy Act. As one commentator noted, "this new legislation may pave a new road to court for class actions in the wake of data breaches affecting California consumers" (Lilley, Weinberg, and Parasharami, 2018). In this scenario, the penalties that the rental car company would face if subject to the GDPR would be a function of various factors, including the scope of the breach, the rental car company's revenue, and whether the rental car company disclosed the breach within 72 hours.[20] In addition, the U.S. Supreme Court decision in *Carpenter* (discussed in the "Privacy Laws" section of Chapter Six) makes it more likely that geolocation information would be considered to be highly sensitive in data security litigation. Although no civil liability cases based on *Carpenter* have been brought, they will likely be filed in the future. As noted above, the plaintiffs' lawyers have indicated their intention to cite *Carpenter* in support of arguments that location information is highly sensitive. In short, under the recent *Carpenter* decision and privacy statutes and regulations, the rental car company could face very serious consequences if personal information was breached.

While causes of action under a negligence theory, an invasion of privacy theory, and potentially a trade secrets theory would also be available to plaintiffs whose private information was stolen, plaintiffs may face hurdles in proving actionable injury and proximate causation under these theories in the absence of misuse of their private information. Despite hurdles, it is possible to establish standing to bring claims arising from a data breach even absent evidence of actual harm caused by the breach. For example, in a case against Adobe Systems Inc. arising from data breach and theft of plaintiffs' usernames, passwords, email addresses, and other information, the court found that the plaintiffs had standing to bring a lawsuit even though they could not allege actual misuse of their stolen personal information ("Adobe

---

19 AB 375 (2017–2018).

20 See Marr, 2018.

Data Breach Ruling Gives New Hope to Plaintiffs," 2014).[21] In addition, as demonstrated by the massive settlement in the Target litigation (Cooney and Kurane, 2015), potential for considerable damages and reputational loss might propel the rental car company to settle the lawsuit for a considerable amount of money.

## Scenario Takeaways

These four scenarios highlight several issues relevant to potential plaintiffs and defendants.

### Vehicle and Component Part Manufacturers

In the context of cyberattacks on AVs, negligence will likely play a prominent role in lawsuits against vehicle and component part manufacturers. In making negligence determinations, courts will consider whether similar attacks have occurred so that manufacturer defendants could have foreseen that failure to take precautions against similar attacks would allow similar attacks. Manufacturers of vehicles and component parts will need to stay abreast of attacks on AVs and take any necessary precautions to avoid similar attacks if they wish to avoid lawsuits. In addition, in making negligence determinations, courts will likely consider whether the costs of adopting alternative technology that is less vulnerable to attacks or other precautionary measures are outweighed by the risks involved with not taking the measure. To prevail, manufacturers will need to convince the court that costs of alternative technologies are prohibitive (i.e., the costs of adopting alternative technology that is less vulnerable to attacks outweigh the costs of damages resulting from the attacks) or that better technology is nonexistent. Manufacturers will likely need to hire experts to assist them in familiarizing the court with the technology at issue and the costs of allegedly superior technology. Experts will be particularly important in the early years of lawsuits arising from cyberattacks, when courts will have less experience in the autonomous realm. In addition,

[21] The Adobe lawsuit was ultimately settled (Grande, 2015).

other civil liability theories that will likely play a role in lawsuits arising from cyberattacks on AVs will require courts to undertake cost-benefit analyses: Many courts use a cost-benefit or risk-utility test to determine whether a design is defective under a strict liability theory. Furthermore, under many state unfair and deceptive practices statutes, plaintiffs have to prove that defendants engaged in conduct that caused them or other consumers substantial injury, that the injury could not be reasonably avoided, and that the potential harm was not outweighed by countervailing benefits to consumers. As AV manufacturers develop customs with respect to minimizing vulnerability of parts and systems to cyberattacks, courts will also take these customs into account when making negligence determinations. Thus, it is important that manufacturers stay informed of and comply with industry standards if they wish to prevail on negligence claims.

### Local and State Governments

If an attack causes damage to government property, the government, as a plaintiff, may recover damages for harm to property but likely not for rescue efforts related to the attack. Assuming that the government is unable to identify the hacker and instead brings a negligence suit against vehicle or component part manufacturers, a court would undertake the same negligence analysis that it would for a private defendant (e.g., is there evidence of breach of a cybersecurity standard, or are the costs of adopting an alternate technology outweighed by risks involved in not adopting the technology? Was the attack foreseeable by the defendants?). Governments might also be defendants in lawsuits involving cyberattacks—for example, if an attacker hacks into the city's stoplight system. Governments will likely be immune from suit if a court considers the government responsibility at issue to be discretionary as opposed to ministerial. Discretionary functions involve significant public policy decisionmaking. As AVs and supporting infrastructure develop, government agencies will be more likely to be held civilly liable if their negligence provides the attacker an opportunity to cause a crash. Lawsuits based on negligence would also involve the same analyses undertaken with respect to private defendants. For example, the court would likely reference safety standards for governments to determine whether a government breached a duty of care.

### Owners and Operators

If an owner or operator of a vehicle sues the manufacturer of a vehicle or component part under a negligence theory after a cyberattack on their AV, the owner or operator will have to prove that the manufacturer's negligence was the cause of their injury. If the owner rejected an important security update that would have prevented the attack, then a court may hold that the owner's negligence in rejecting the update was the cause of the owner's injury.[22] In addition, a plaintiff would have to identify a precaution that each defendant could have taken to avoid the attack (e.g., the car manufacturer should have incorporated specific alternate technology to prevent the cyberattack) and show that the costs of adopting alternative technology that is less vulnerable to attacks or other precautionary measures are outweighed by risks involved with not taking the measure. Thus, when owners and operators are plaintiffs in lawsuits arising from cyberattacks, they will also likely need to make use of experts. As noted above, experts will be particularly important in the early years of lawsuits arising from cyberattacks, when courts will have less experience in the autonomous realm. As plaintiffs, owners and operators will need to demonstrate that the costs of superior technology that would be less susceptible to an attack are outweighed by the harm caused by the attack to prevail on claims based on negligence and design defect theories, as well as claims based on common consumer protection statutes. Plaintiffs should carefully choose experts and develop strategies to optimize their use.[23]

---

[22] Although owners and operators are more likely to take no action than to affirmatively reject an update or patch, nonaction is very rarely grounds for common law liability unless there is a clear duty to act. This is why lawmakers and policymakers have considered regulations that require AV owners to install updates. See, e.g., Williams, 2017.

[23] However, note that there may be some instances when an expert would not be necessary to demonstrate liability. For example, as discussed in Restatement (Third) of Torts: Prods. Liab. § 2 cmt. f., plaintiffs in design defect cases may be able to prove a design defect without the use of an expert:

"While a plaintiff must prove that a reasonable alternative design would have reduced the foreseeable risks of harm, Subsection (b) does not require the plaintiff to produce expert testimony in every case. Cases arise in which the feasibility of a reasonable alternative design is obvious and understandable to laypersons and therefore expert testimony is unnecessary to support a finding that the product should have been designed differently and more safely. For example, when a manufacturer sells a soft stuffed toy with hard plastic buttons that are easily removable and likely to choke and suffocate a small child who foreseeably attempts to swallow them, the plaintiff should be able to reach the trier of fact with a claim that buttons on such a toy should be an integral part of the toy's fabric itself (or otherwise be unremovable by an infant) without hiring an expert to demonstrate the feasibility of an alternative safer design. Furthermore, other products already available on the market may serve the same or very similar function at lower risk and at comparable cost. Such products may serve as reasonable alternatives to the product in question."

CHAPTER EIGHT

# Conclusions

The following numbers herald the (eventual) approach of the era of AVs: Thousands of autonomous driving patents are being sought (Cavanaugh et al., 2017). Tens of billions of dollars of corporate and venture capital funding are committed to the development of AV technology (Viereckl et al., 2016). In the United States alone, 163 companies are betting on a driverless future ("Autonomy Is Driving a Surge of Auto Tech Investment," 2017). Beyond such economic interests in AVs, popular culture's fascination with driverless cars points to the enormous societal interest in the technology. This interest is driven in part by AVs' promise of significant benefits to social welfare—if policymakers handle the transition to driverless cars in such a way that mitigates downsides (Anderson et al., 2016). As with any new technology, however, AVs pose risks that must be predicted and prepared for.

Along with such concerns as economic displacement of professional drivers, the threat of hackers commandeering AVs is attracting the interest of researchers and the AV industry. The specter of tens of thousands of cars running amok at the bidding of malicious hackers should give policymakers and AV advocates pause even if its likelihood is small. This preliminary investigation has explored aspects of that specter: the nature of AVs and connected roadways, their cyber vulnerabilities, the physical damage that could result from successful hacks, the civil liability implications of such events, and how the roles of stakeholders may change in an AV future. Adoption of the technology and its ability to pay social dividends depend in part not only on the substance of those risks but also on the *perception* of those risks and the legal structures that might compensate for them. Even if the risks are small, policymakers will need to anticipate and react to them to secure the potential societal benefits of AVs.

The authors reviewed the cyber vulnerabilities of AVs and the connected roadways they may transit and confirmed that hackers will have multiple avenues of attack on AVs. Those attacks may attempt to exploit not just the processors in cars and transportation systems but also all the communications channels likely to accompany AVs. That includes servers and networks operated by manufacturers, car dealers, repair shops, financial services companies that facilitate owning and renting cars, regulators, insurers, aftermarket parts suppliers, and their respective third-party cloud providers. Due to the common network and software systems that AVs likely will use, hackers could be able to scale up their attacks in terms of intensity (e.g., attacks can scale from disabling a car for ransom to mowing down pedestrians), and hackers could scale out their attacks in terms of breadth (i.e., they could potentially hack all the cars with common architecture to disable them or use them as instruments of destruction). Hacks could also take the form of data theft, a plague already familiar to information assurance professionals.

The damages that hacked AVs could inflict range from familiar privacy or financial hacking losses to the physical destruction that current vehicles can inflict. Given AVs' capacity for remote control, they may even enable harms in the physical world that currently do not take place because of the difficulty of finding drivers willing to put themselves at risk during ramming or crash-and-grab attacks.

These kinds of cyber risks and technological advances will likely shuffle the roles and responsibilities for information assurance among stakeholders in the AV ecosystem. Those stakeholders include

- creators and manufacturers (of cars, hardware, and software)
- supply chain providers (of components or intellectual property)
- service providers (e.g., consultants, contractors, bankers, repair shop owners and employees, lawyers)
- competitors (in the development, market offering, and service life phases)

- dealers and aftermarket installers (of cars and parts)
- users (e.g., passengers who are not paying)
- customers (e.g., car purchasers or payers)
- owners (individuals or corporations)
- operators (individuals or corporations)
- insurers
- regulators.

On the whole, this analysis indicates that the roles of some stakeholders in information assurance may lengthen and intensify compared with the current auto industry model. For example, manufacturers currently hand off responsibility for routine maintenance items like oil changes to the owners themselves or repair shops. Manufacturers may retain greater control of, and responsibility for, information assurance if they take advantage of over-the-air software updates to improve an AV's features.[1] That same lengthening and intensification of information assurance responsibilities could affect companies that sell or lease AVs.

AVs, and the hacking threats that will accompany them, also place the roles and responsibilities of individual car owners (and passengers in cars operated by ride-for-hire companies) in a new light. For instance, can individual owners or passengers reasonably be expected to detect hacks? Or even ensure that software updates are current? Regulators may need to identify which responsibilities can reasonably be placed on individual owners or passengers. They also may need to determine whether any form of licensure is appropriate for individual owners of AVs; even if they never expect to take the wheel, such owners may need to demonstrate some kind of general training in responsible AV ownership.

On the general question of civil liability for cyberattacks on AVs and their accompanying infrastructure, our analysis yielded multiple findings that may be of interest to stakeholders:

---

1 See Smith (2013).

- AV manufacturers, manufacturers and designers of component parts and software, and distributors of AVs may face civil liability for the criminal hacks on AVs.
- Drivers of AVs may also face liability for cyberattacks if, for example, they reject an important security update that allows a hacker to take control of the AV and steer it into another vehicle.
- Existing civil liability law will likely be sufficiently flexible to adapt to hacked AV liability claims, at least for small- and medium-scale attacks.
- Negligence, product liability laws, warranty law, and state and federal privacy laws are likely to be the most relevant bodies of law in lawsuits arising specifically from cyberattacks on AVs.
- Because of the role of foreseeability in determinations of liability for the criminal acts of a third party (like hacking), the issue of prior exploitation of a vulnerability of a component part or system in an AV will likely play a key role in liability determinations under existing civil liability law.
- Negligence and product liability will likely play a prominent role in lawsuits against AV and component part manufacturers. Cost-benefit and foreseeability analyses thus will influence legal analysis of responsibility for damages from cyberattacks.
  - These cost-benefit analyses will require courts to become familiar with the technology at issue.
  - Manufacturers of vehicles and component parts would need to stay abreast of attacks on AVs and take any necessary precautions to avoid similar attacks if they wish to avoid liability.
- Government agencies will be potential defendants in civil lawsuits that arise out of incidents involving unsafe infrastructure and will likely be protected by sovereign immunity as they adapt roadways to AVs. That immunity may not apply as they undertake ministerial tasks like road maintenance. Thus, after AVs and supporting infrastructure develop, government agencies will be more likely to be held civilly liable if their negligence provides the attacker an opportunity to cause a crash. Considerable state-by-state variation in sovereign immunity doctrine complicates the analysis.

As indicated above, existing civil legal frameworks are likely to adapt to new factual and legal circumstances created by widespread introduction of AVs. However, that does not prevent policymakers from considering whether statutory approaches that define roles and responsibilities would facilitate adoption of the technology. Such a statutory framework might offer the benefit of clarifying duties but may seem inflexible when compared with the common law system in the face of both hard-to-anticipate technological developments and novel fact patterns.

Similarly, it would be helpful to better understand and perhaps clarify insurance coverage for cyberattacks on AVs for both consumer and commercial policies so that consumers, automakers, and policymakers can better understand which parties will bear the costs of such attacks.

Policymakers may also want to carefully consider how the legal system might cope with a large-scale attack. Such an attack could lead to bankruptcies and uncompensated losses and could exceed the capacity of insurers and reinsurers to cover the risk. Somewhat similar concerns in the wake of the September 11, 2001, attacks led to the passage of the Terrorism Risk Insurance Act.[2] A similar approach may be warranted for this set of risks.

The exploratory analysis in this report provides a framework for policymakers tasked with maximizing the benefits of AVs (and minimizing the potential harms from hacked AVs) to sort out roles and responsibilities in an AV future. It also offers parties with a stake in the AV future considerations as to how their roles and responsibilities may change as the technology spreads through the road system. This discussion lays the groundwork for further analysis of how those roles and responsibilities may evolve.

Unfortunately, we have grown all too accustomed to the occasional hack of some of our personal information. Human beings are not very good at rationally anticipating low-probability events. And the consequences of most consumer hacks are relatively mild—on the order of inconvenience rather than tragedy. Perhaps not surprisingly,

---

2 See Dixon et al. (2014).

cybersecurity breaches have not led to a strong consumer demand for increased cybersecurity (Ablon et al., 2016). Thus far, consumers have shrugged, changed their passwords, and moved on. Hacked AVs, however, threaten a range of consequences that vastly exceed those of most consumer hacks to date. It will be interesting to see whether those heightened consequences create strong consumer incentives for cybersecurity of AVs.

APPENDIX A

# Cyber Exploits Against Autonomous Vehicles

Security of AVs has received considerable recent attention. Several studies have explored potential cyberattacks on such systems and provide proofs of concept of successful attacks on components of AVs. This appendix reviews some of those studies to provide a framework for deeper understanding of possible cyberattacks on AVs.

This discussion distinguishes passive attacks from active attacks. Passive attacks are those where the vehicle is tricked into taking a wrong decision. Active attacks are those where the vehicle is explicitly directed or forced to make a wrong decision. While this distinction is not clear in many of the cases listed in the tables below, we believe it may have implications for liability analysis. In any case, this distinctions help provide a structure to this section.

## Active Attacks

Koscher et al. (2010) have carried out an experimental analysis of the cybersecurity of modern automobiles. Although their research does not necessarily look at the security of AVs, their experimental results are still highly relevant to AVs because many of the components they analyze are common to most modern vehicles, including AVs. Using lab experiments and road tests, the authors demonstrate that a hacker with an ability to infiltrate any of the ECUs of a vehicle can circumvent the safety-critical systems to gain control of many functions of the vehicle. All the experiments carried out presume that the attacker has already exploited vulnerabilities and gained access to the components of the vehicle.

Below we summarize some of the kinds of attacks on a few important ECUs that Koscher et al. (2010) were able to successfully demonstrate. Along with each kind of attack, we provide the mechanism used to launch the attack and some of the plausible consequences of those attacks.

### Demonstrated Attacks on the Body Control Module

The body control module (BCM) is the ECU responsible for controlling the functionality of various automated components that form the body of the vehicle. The functionality of such components as power windows, power door locks, windshield wipers, the trunk, brake lights, and others are all controlled by the BCM. Table A.1 captures different kinds of attacks that were demonstrated on the BCM.

**Table A.1**
**Attacks on the Body Control Module and Their Plausible Consequences**

| Description of the Attack | Mechanism of Attack | Plausible Consequences | Severity of Consequences |
|---|---|---|---|
| Continuously activates lock relay | Repeatedly sending an instruction | Door locks of the car constantly alternate between locked and unlocked state | Low to medium |
| Runs windshield wipers continuously | Repeatedly sending an instruction | Affects passenger visibility of the road | Low |
| Pops trunk | One-time instruction | Affects passenger visibility of the road; potential damage to goods stored in the trunk | Low to medium |
| Releases shift lock solenoid | One-time instruction | Sets the vehicle in free motion | Medium to high |
| Unlocks all doors | One-time instruction | Threatens passenger safety | Low to high |
| Permanently activates horn | Repeatedly sending an instruction | Annoyance | Low |

**Table A.1—continued**

| Description of the Attack | Mechanism of Attack | Plausible Consequences | Severity of Consequences |
|---|---|---|---|
| Disables headlights in auto light control | One-time instruction | Makes identification of the vehicle difficult for others on the road | Low to high |
| Turns all auxiliary lights off | One-time instruction | Makes identification of the vehicle difficult for others on the road | Low to high |
| Disables window and key lock relays | One-time instruction | Windows and locks may become dysfunctional and remain in the same state until the relays are enabled | Low to medium |
| Sprays windshield fluid continuously | Repeatedly sending an instruction | Affects passenger visibility of the road | Low to medium |
| Controls horn frequency | Data manipulation and one-time instruction | Annoyance | Low to medium |
| Controls dome light brightness | Data manipulation and one-time instruction | Annoyance | Low to medium |
| Controls instrument brightness | Data manipulation and one-time instruction | Annoyance | Low to medium |
| Turns all brake and auxiliary lights off | One-time instruction | Makes identification of the vehicle difficult for others on the road | Low to high |
| Forces wipers off and sprays windshield fluid continuously | One-time instruction and repeatedly sending an instruction | Affects passenger visibility of the road | Low to medium |

SOURCE: Derived from Koscher et al. (2010).

### Demonstrated Attacks on the Engine Control Module

The engine control module (ECM) of a vehicle is the ECU that controls the functionality of the engine. The ECM decides what action to perform based on the information it receives from various sensors. Table A.2 catalogs the attacks on the ECM and the plausible consequences.

### Demonstrated Attacks on the Electronic Brake Control Module

The electronic brake control module (EBCM) is the ECU that is responsible for controlling the antilock brake system (ABS) of the vehicle. The ABS usually prevents the vehicle from skidding due to sudden locking of brakes. It does so by regulating the hydraulic pressure on the brakes. This unit, like all other units, was attacked in two different settings; we mention the two different settings explicitly for this case because it has varying results in both the settings. In the first

**Table A.2**
**Attacks on the Engine Control Module and Their Plausible Consequences**

| Description of the Attack | Mechanism of Attack | Plausible Consequences | Severity of Consequences |
|---|---|---|---|
| Initiates crankshaft re-learn; disturbs timing | One-time instruction and data manipulation | Loss in fuel efficiency; ignition failure | Low to medium |
| Increases RPM temporarily | Repeated instruction and data manipulation | Variation in speed of the vehicle | Low to high |
| Disables cylinders, power steering, and brakes | One-time instruction | Ignition failure | Low to medium |
| Kills engine, causes knocking on restart | One-time instruction | Ignition failure | Low to medium |
| Grinds starter | One-time instruction | Annoyance; grinding noise when key turn initiates ignition | Low |
| Increases idle RPM | Repeated instruction | Annoyance; waste of fuel | Low |

SOURCE: Derived from Koscher et al. (2010).

NOTE: RPM = revolutions per minute.

setting, the car was kept stationary on a jack stand, and in the second setting, the car was in motion on a runway. When the car was on the jack stand, all the attacks went through without the need to unlock the device using the DeviceControl key (the DeviceControl key can be thought of as a password to unlock the device). However, when the car was in motion and at a speed higher than 5 mph, the car rejected the malicious instructions if the device was not unlocked using the DeviceControl key. Once the device was unlocked using the appropriate DeviceControl key, all the attacks were successful. See Table A.3.

### Demonstrated Attacks on Some Other Modules

Attacks were also carried out, in general, on other modules using reverse engineering techniques. It was surprisingly easy, the researchers noted, to reverse engineer these modules to figure out what instructions to send and what data to manipulate in order to achieve a successful attack. These exploitations needed more sophistication than the other attacks discussed. However, the severity levels of these attacks are lower than those of some of the previously discussed attacks. See Table A.4.

**Table A.3**
**Attacks on the Electronic Brake Control Module and Their Plausible Consequences**

| Description of the Attack | Mechanism of Attack | Plausible Consequences | Severity of Consequences |
|---|---|---|---|
| Engages front left brake and unlocks front right brake | One-time instruction | Vehicle jerks, may swivel left | Low to high |
| Engages front right brake and unlocks front left brake | One-time instruction | Vehicle jerks, may swivel right | Low to high |
| Unevenly engages right brakes | One-time instruction | Unexpected jerks and swivels | Low to high |
| Releases brakes, prevents braking | Repeated instructions | Does not stop; may cause a crash | Low to high |

SOURCE: Derived from Koscher et al. (2010).

**Table A.4**
**Other Miscellaneous Attacks and Their Plausible Consequences**

| Description of the Attack | Mechanism of Attack | Plausible Consequences | Severity of Consequences |
|---|---|---|---|
| Falsifies speedometer reading | Data manipulation | Misinformation to the passenger in the car | Low |
| Increases radio volume | Data manipulation | Annoyance | Low |
| Changes radio display | Data manipulation | Annoyance | Low |
| Changes digital instrument display | Data manipulation | Annoyance | Low |
| Unlocks car | One-time instruction | Annoyance | Low |
| Locks car | One-time instruction | Annoyance | Low |
| Remotely starts car | One-time instruction | Annoyance | Low |
| Triggers car alarm | One-time instruction | Annoyance | Low |
| Triggers ticking sound | One-time instruction | Annoyance | Low |
| Kills engine | One-time instruction | Annoyance | Low |

SOURCE: Derived from Koscher et al. (2010).

## What Enables These Attacks?

It is important to note that these attacks are enabled in part because of the way the CAN is designed and implemented as a standard for communication between various components of a vehicle. Those design and implementation decisions have been interpreted as "weaknesses of the CAN protocol" by Yağdereli, Gemci, and Aktaş (2015). The specific weaknesses of the CAN protocol they refer to are discussed below.

One weakness is that messages sent using the CAN protocol are broadcast to all devices connected to the CAN. Thus, any entity connected to the CAN can receive every message that has been sent using the protocol. This can enable a malicious or a compromised entity to capture a message sent to some other device, reengineer it, and send a malicious message to another entity directing it to take an action that was not warranted.

A second weakness is that the CAN protocol is vulnerable to a DoS attack. In this scenario, an entity can keep sending messages incessantly over the CAN, thereby denying the use of the CAN by other entities connected to the network.

A third weakness of the CAN protocol is that it has no scope for authentication of messages sent over the CAN because there are no designated authenticator fields. This implies that any malicious entity with access to the CAN can pretend to be some other entity and send a message over the CAN. It is up to the connected components to defend against such unauthorized messages received over the CAN.

A fourth weakness is the support for diagnostics and testing over the CAN. The diagnostics and testing capabilities are very important for mechanics and technicians when troubleshooting whether something is wrong with the vehicle. However, a malicious actor can exploit these capabilities to launch an attack on one or more components connected to the CAN.

Because the weaknesses described above can also be viewed as minimalistic features that enable faster operations over the CAN, there could be significant challenges in assessing liability if a successful attack is launched after exploiting one or more of these weaknesses.

## Passive Attacks

Petit and Shladover (2015) provide a good list of plausible cyberattacks on AVs. In order to come up with a list of attacks on AVs, the authors used a methodology that is a very close variant of the failure mode effects analysis method used in designing and engineering a system that is resilient to failure. They examined the important components of the AV (and other components they interacted with in the ecosystem) to assess some of the plausible cyber vulnerabilities and determine what hazards could be created if those vulnerabilities are exploited. Broad themes of attacks found in their analysis are described in Table A.5.

The attacks described by Petit and Shladover (2015) are mostly passive in nature (letting the vehicle make a wrong decision or tricking it into doing so) as opposed to the active attacks described in Koscher et al. (2010) (directing or forcing the vehicle to make wrong decisions). Transportation infrastructure may be exploited and the data that the infrastructure provides to vehicles for safe and disciplined transportation may be manipulated to trick AVs into taking actions they otherwise would not have taken. Although these attacks are not on the vehicle itself, this is an important category of attacks that may complicate analysis of legal liability in case of a successful attack. Blinding and spoofing attacks have been common on electronic components. When these attacks are carried out on AVs, they could result in crashes, not just violations of traffic laws. The same holds for the attacks on GPS. Another important category of attacks is data theft, which may result in loss of privacy of individuals who may own or use AVs. This kind of attack can be executed by stealing the data captured by in-vehicle

**Table A.5**
**Attacks on Components of Autonomous Vehicles and Other Transportation Infrastructure**

| Description of the Attack | Mechanism of Attack | Plausible Consequences | Severity of Consequences |
|---|---|---|---|
| Manipulates the signs of transportation infrastructure | Data manipulation (infrastructure, not the vehicle) | Violation of traffic laws, traffic disturbance, crash | Low to high |
| Blinds and spoofs the vehicle's sensors | Overprovision of data; fake data | Violation of traffic laws, traffic disturbance, crash | Low to high |
| Spoofs and jams the GPS device | Fake signals; overprovision of signals | Vehicle may halt; vehicle drives to a wrong destination; crash | Low to high |
| Exploits in-vehicle sensors for eavesdropping | Data theft | Loss of privacy; enables future attacks | Low to medium |

SOURCE: Derived from Petit and Shladover (2015).

sensors, such as voice recorders and Bluetooth devices. The data could be used to stalk the individuals by analyzing the movement patterns of individuals using the AV. While this is not an attack that necessarily tricks the vehicle into making a wrong decision, it is nevertheless a passive form of attack.

**How Can an Attacker Get Access to the In-Vehicle Network?**

Until now, we have proceeded under the assumption that an attacker has already secured access to the in-vehicle network and was able to launch some of the attacks described above. The remainder of this appendix explores whether the assumption is reasonable. In order to assess whether the assumption is reasonable, we reviewed some of the experimental studies that have been carried out to explore whether an attacker can get access to the in-vehicle network.

Literature related to getting unauthorized access to the CAN is scarce, and we did not find many reliable studies. Some studies provided reasonable conjectures based on in-depth analysis of the internal organizations (and interconnections) of various ECUs of vehicles. One such study was presented by Miller and Valasek at the Black Hat conference held in Las Vegas in 2014 (Miller and Valasek, undated). From the analysis provided in their report, it is apparent that ECUs connected to the CAN do not have many records of being hacked, and the ECUs that have a history of being hacked are, in many cases, not connected to the CAN. This might be one of the strongest factors explaining why hacking into a vehicle to get access to its in-vehicle networks has not been a frequent phenomenon. Nevertheless, their analysis did find some vehicles in which vulnerable ECUs were connected to the CAN. Theoretically speaking, by hacking one of those ECUs, an attacker could obtain unauthorized access to the CAN, through which they then could execute several of the attacks described above.

The Bluetooth ECU, the cellular network telematics ECU, and the infotainment system ECU have at least a plausible potential of being hacked into. Jacobson and Wetzel (2001) provide a very detailed analysis of the security weaknesses of the Bluetooth stack. Some of the cellular network telematics ECUs in a few cars analyzed by Miller and Valasek (undated) contained Qualcomm chips. At the 2016 Black

Hat conference, Israeli cybersecurity firm Checkpoint presented four flaws in certain chips produced by Qualcomm that could be exploited to get complete access to the device on which the chip was mounted (Kuchler, 2016). Many of the advanced infotainment systems had many different applications installed, such as internet browsers and media players. These kinds of software are known for being vulnerable to exploitation. This shows that it is at least plausible that an attacker could hack into one of the ECUs to get unauthorized access to the in-vehicle networks.

APPENDIX B

# The Phases of the National Institute of Standards and Technology Cyber-Physical System Draft Framework

**Table B.1**
**National Institute of Standards and Technology Cyber-Physical System Framework, with Additions**

| Product Phase | CPS Facets | Stakeholder Classes | Key Security Challenges |
|---|---|---|---|
| 1. Development and production | Conceptualization + realization + assurance | • Creators/ manufacturers<br>• Supply chain providers<br>• Service providers (consultants, contractors)<br>• Competitors | • Ongoing feature development on released models for competitiveness<br>• Machine-to-machine communication security<br>• Protection of authentication key/certificates for features beyond driving |
| 2. Market offering | Realization + assurance | • Dealers/aftermarket installation (the public/society)<br>• Customers/ payers<br>• Service providers<br>• Bankers<br>• Competitors | • Protection of AV delivery channels<br>• Owner/user segmentation of security product offerings<br>• Information assurance agreements |

**Table B.1—continued**

| Product Phase | CPS Facets | Stakeholder Classes | Key Security Challenges |
|---|---|---|---|
| 3. Transportation service life | Assurance (individual focused) | • Owners<br>• Operators<br>• Customers/ users<br>• Service providers<br>• Repair/service shops<br>• Competitors | • Shared versus consolidated maintenance roles<br>• Protection of repair service facilities<br>• Monitoring of new service marketing claims |
| 4. Market protection | Assurance (society focused) | • Service providers<br>• Lawyers<br>• Insurers<br>• Regulators<br>• Government | • Risk mitigation framework<br>• Vehicle safety/ security certification<br>• User training/ certification<br>• Monitoring data sharing with infrastructure |

# Bibliography

28 U.S.C. § 1346.

28 U.S.C. § 2680(a).

49 U.S.C. § 30111(a).

AB 375, 2017–2018. As of June 18, 2019:
https://leginfo.legislature.ca.gov/faces/billTextClient.xhtml?bill_id=201720180AB375

Ablon, Lillian, Paul Heaton, Diana Catherine Lavery, and Sasha Romanosky, *Consumer Attitudes Toward Data Breach Notifications and Loss of Personal Information*, Santa Monica, Calif.: RAND Corporation, RR-1187-ICJ, 2016. As of May 7, 2019:
https://www.rand.org/pubs/research_reports/RR1187.html

Acker, A., and B. Beaton, "Software Update Unrest: The Recent Happenings Around Tinder and Tesla," *49th Hawaii International Conference on System Sciences (HICSS)*, Koloa, Hawaii, 2016, pp. 1891–1900. As of June 22, 2017:
https://www.computer.org/csdl/proceedings/hicss/2016/5670/00/index.html

Adams, A., "Man Says Tesla Car Started on Its Own, Crashed into Trailer," *KSL.com*, May 11, 2016. As of June 19, 2018:
https://www.ksl.com/?sid=39727592&nid=148&title=utah-man-says-tesla-car-started-on-its-own-crashed-into-trailer

"Adobe Data Breach Ruling Gives New Hope to Plaintiffs," *Law 360*, September 24, 2014. As of July 3, 2018:
http://www.law360.com/articles/579164/adobe-data-breach-ruling-gives-new-hope-to-plaintiffs

*Almazan v. CTB, Inc.*, No. CIV.A.SA-99-CA355PMA, 2000 WL 33348244, at *10, W.D. Tex., April 27, 2000.

*Am. Aviation*, 891 So. 2d, 2004.

*Am. Motors Corp. v. Ellis*, 403 So. 2d 459, Fla. Dist. Ct. App., 1981.

Anderson, James M., Nidhi Kalra, Karlyn D. Stanley, Paul Sorensen, Constantine Samaras, and Tobi A. Oluwatola, *Autonomous Vehicle Technology: A Guide for Policymakers*, Santa Monica, Calif.: RAND Corporation, RR-443-2-RC, 2016. As of May 7, 2019:
http://www.rand.org/pubs/research_reports/RR443-2.html

*Ann M. v. Pacific Plaza Shopping Center*, 863 P.2d 207, Cal., 1993.

Associated Press, "Video Shows Google Self-Driving Car Hit Bus," March 9, 2016. As of June 17, 2019:
https://www.youtube.com/watch?v=neFqatFxwnw

Atherton, K., "ISIS Shows Off a Driverless Carbomb," *Popular Science*, January 6, 2016. As of June 23, 2017:
http://www.popsci.com/isis-shows-off-driverless-carbomb

Auto-ISAC—*See* Automotive Information Sharing and Analysis Center.

Automotive Information Sharing and Analysis Center, homepage, 2019. As of June 19, 2019:
https://www.automotiveisac.com

"Autonomy Is Driving a Surge of Auto Tech Investment," *CB Insights*, November 16, 2017. As of July 3, 2018:
https://www.cbinsights.com/research/auto-tech-startup-investment-trends/

Beck, J. M., and M. D. Jacobson, "3D Printing: What Could Happen to Products Liability When Users (and Everyone Else in Between) Become Manufacturers," *Minnesota Journal of Law, Science, and Technology*, Vol. 18, No. 1, 2017, pp. 143–205.

Bodeau, D., R. Graubart, and J. Fabius, *Improving Cyber Security and Mission Assurance via Cyber Preparedness (Cyber Prep) Levels*, MITRE, February 2010. As of June 23, 2017:
https://www.mitre.org/publications/technical-papers/improving-cyber-security-and-mission-assurance-via-cyber-preparedness-cyber-prep-levels

Boeglin, Jack, "The Costs of Self-Driving Cars: Reconciling Freedom and Privacy with Tort Liability in Autonomous Vehicle Regulation," *Yale Journal of Law and Technology*, Vol. 17, No. 1, 2015.

Bolon, A.-S., P. Karasz, and J. C. McKinley, Jr., "Van Hits Pedestrians in Deadly Barcelona Terror Attack," *New York Times*, August 17, 2017. As of June 19, 2018:
https://www.nytimes.com/2017/08/17/world/europe/barcelona-catalunya-van.html?_r=0

Bulwa, D., and P. Fimrite, "Tanker Fire Destroys Part of MacArthur Maze/2 Freeways Closed Near Bay Bridge," *SFGate*, April 29, 2007. As of June 23, 2017:
http://www.sfgate.com/bayarea/article/Tanker-fire-destroys-part-of-MacArthur-Maze-2-2575285.php

*Cahen v. Toyota Motor Corp.*, 147 F. Supp. 3d 955, N.D. Cal., 2015.

*Cahen v. Toyota Motor Corp.*, No. 16-15496, 9th Cir., December 21, 2017.

California Code of Regulations, Title 13, Division 1, Chapter 1, Article 3.7 ("Testing of Autonomous Vehicles").

California Department of Motor Vehicles, "CA DMV §228.06. Application for a Permit for Post-Testing Deployment of Autonomous Vehicles on Public Roads," undated. As of June 19, 2018:
https://www.dmv.ca.gov/portal/wcm/connect/7342a60f-4953-48e4-9372-51abe905913f/avinitialstatementofreasons_31017.pdf?MOD=AJPERES

Calnan, A., and A. E. Taslitz, "Defusing Bomb-Blast Terrorism: A Legal Survey of Technological and Regulatory Alternatives," *Tennessee Law Review*, Vol. 67, 1999.

*Carpenter v. US*, 585 U.S. ____, 2018.

Carter, C., *Consumer Protection in the States: A 50-State Report on Unfair and Deceptive Acts and Practices Statutes*, Boston, Mass.: National Consumer Law Center, February 2009. As of June 22, 2018:
https://www.nclc.org/images/pdf/udap/report_50_states.pdf

Cavanaugh, D., Y.-H. S. Ha, N. H. Leh, M. Silhasek, and T. Zubler, "Trends in Automotive Technology: 2017 and the Road Ahead," *WilmerHale*, December 22, 2017. As of July 3, 2018:
https://www.wilmerhale.com/en/insights/publications/2017-12-22-trends-in-automotive-technology-2017-and-the-road-ahead

Computer Fraud and Abuse Act, 18 U.S.C. § 1030, 1984.

Connecticut Department of Transportation, *Loss of Business Payments Survey*, undated.

Cooney, P., and S. Kurane, "Target Agrees to Pay $10 Million to Settle Lawsuit from Data Breach," Reuters, 2015. As of July 2, 2018:
http://www.reuters.com/article/us-target-settlement-idUSKBN0MF04K20150319

*Corley v. Stryker Corp.*, No. 6:13-CV-02571, 2014 WL 3375596 at *1, W.D. La, May 27, 2014, adopted.

*Corley v. Stryker Orthopaedics*, No. 13-2571, 2014 WL 3125990, W.D. La., July 3, 2014.

Croft, S., "Who Will Be Liable for Driverless Cars?" *Automotive World*, August 2013. As of June 22, 2018:
http://www.shb.com/~/media/files/professionals/croftsarah/whowillbeliablefordriverlesscars.pdf?la=en

"Dark Motives Online: An Analysis of Overlapping Technologies Used by Cybercriminals and Terrorist Organizations," *Trend Micro*, May 3, 2016. As of June 23, 2017:
https://www.trendmicro.com/vinfo/us/security/news/cybercrime-and-digital-threats/overlapping-technologies-cybercriminals-and-terrorist-organizations

*Davenport v. Nixon*, 434 So. 2d 1203, La. Ct. App., 1983.

Davis, J., *Autonomous and Connected Vehicles: A Law Enforcement Primer*, Monterey, Calif.: Naval Postgraduate School, 2015. As of July 2, 2018:
https://www.hsdl.org/?view&did=790319

de Villiers, M., "Computer Viruses and Civil Liability: A Conceptual Framework," *Tort Trial & Insurance Practice Law Journal*, Vol. 40, No. 1, 2004, pp. 123–179.

de Villiers, M., "Free Radicals in Cyberspace: Complex Liability Issues in Information Warfare," *Northwestern Journal of Technology and Intellectual Property*, Vol. 4, No. 1, 2005, pp. 13–60.

Dearden, L., "Berlin Attack: Lorry's Automatic Braking System Stopped More Deaths During the Christmas Market Assault," *Independent*, December 29, 2016. As of June 23, 2017:
http://www.independent.co.uk/news/world/europe/berlin-attack-truck-isis-automatic-braking-system-deaths-anis-amri-christmas-market-lorry-benefits-a7500591.html

Di Caro, M., "Has the Time Come to Change D.C.'s Contributory Negligence Law for Cyclists?" WAMU Radio, April 21, 2016. As of June 17, 2019:
http://wamu.org/story/16/04/21/has_the_time_come_to_change_dcs_contributory_negligence_law_for_cyclists/

Digital Millennium Copyright Act, 1998.

*District of Columbia v. Air Florida, Inc.*, 750 F.2d 1077, D.C. Cir., 1984.

Dixon, Lloyd, Michael Dworsky, Brian Michael Jenkins, Tom LaTourette, and Henry H. Willis, *The Future of the Terrorism Risk Insurance Act*, Santa Monica, Calif.: RAND Corporation, CF-325-CCRMC, 2014. As of May 7, 2019:
https://www.rand.org/pubs/conf_proceedings/CF325.html

Doherty, Kevin R., "The Art of (Cyber) War," *Policyholder Informer*, blog, February 21, 2017. As of July 3, 2019:
https://policyholderinformer.com/2017/02/21/the-art-of-cyber-war/

DOT—*See* U.S. Department of Transportation.

Doyle, M., "Two Dead After Pursued SUV Crashes into Lemoore Air Base, Hits Fighter Jet," *Fresno Bee*, 2016. As of July 2, 2018:
https://www.fresnobee.com/news/local/article69185952.html

Duffy, S., and J. Hopkins, "Sit, Stay, Drive: The Future of Autonomous Car Liability," *SMU Science and Technology Law Review*, Vol. 16, No. 3, 2013, pp. 453–480.

Dunning, J. P., "Taming the Blue Beast: A Survey of Bluetooth Based Threats," *IEEE Security & Privacy*, Vol. 8, No. 2, March–April 2010, pp. 20–27.

Electronic Communications Privacy Act, 18 U.S.C. §§ 2510–2511, 2012.

Eno Center for Transportation, *Adopting and Adapting: States and Automated Vehicles*, Washington, D.C., 2017. As of June 29, 2018:
https://www.enotrans.org/etl-material/adopting-adapting-states-automated-vehicles/

European Union GDPR—*See* European Union General Data Protection Regulation Portal.

European Union General Data Protection Regulation Portal, homepage, undated. As of June 18, 2019:
https://www.eugdpr.org/

*Evangelical United Brethren Church v. State*, 407 P.2d 440, Wash., 1966.

Evans, W., "Uber Said It Protects You from Spying. Security Sources Say Otherwise," *Reveal News*, December 12, 2016. As of June 23, 2017:
https://www.revealnews.org/article/uber-said-it-protects-you-from-spying-security-sources-say-otherwise/

Executive Order 13693, "Planning for Federal Sustainability in the Next Decade," *Federal Register*, Vol. 80, March 25, 2015, pp. 15869–15884.

Federal Aviation Administration, "No Drone Zone," June 14, 2016. As of June 23, 2017:
https://www.faa.gov/uas/where_to_fly/no_drone_zone/

Fiegerman, S., "Facebook, Google, Twitter Accused of Enabling ISIS," *CNN Tech*, December 20, 2016. As of June 23, 2017:
http://money.cnn.com/2016/12/20/technology/twitter-facebook-google-lawsuit-isis/

*Flynn et al. v. American Honda Motor Co. Inc.*, No. 4:11-cv-3908, S.D. Tex., 2015.

*Flynn v. FCA US LLC*, No. 3: 15-cv 855, S.D. Ill., 2015.

*Forsyth v. Eli Lilly & Co.*, 904 F. Supp. 1153, D. Haw., 1995.

Fraade-Blanar, Laura, Marjory S. Blumenthal, James M. Anderson, and Nidhi Kalra, *Measuring Automated Vehicle Safety: Forging a Framework*, Santa Monica, Calif.: RAND Corporation, RR-2882, 2018. As of June 28, 2019:
https://www.rand.org/pubs/research_reports/RR2662.html

Funkhouser, K., "Paving the Road Ahead: Autonomous Vehicles, Products Liability, and the Need for a New Approach," *Utah Law Review*, Vol. 1, 2013, pp. 437–462.

Galligan Jr., T., P. Haddon, F. Maraist, F. McClellan, M. Rustad, N. Terry, and S. Wildman, *Tort Law: Cases, Perspectives, and Problems*, revised fourth ed., LexisNexis, 2007.

Ganor, B., *The Counter-Terrorism Puzzle: A Guide for Decision Makers*, Piscataway, N.J.: Transaction Publishers, 2005.

Garza, A., "'Look Ma, No Hands!': Wrinkles and Wrecks in the Age of Autonomous Vehicles," *New England Law Review*, Vol. 46, 2012, pp. 581–616.

Gasser, T., "Rechtsfolgen Zunehmender Fahrzeugautomatisierung," *Bast-Bericht*, Vol. F 83, 2012.

Geistfeld, M. A., "A Roadmap for Autonomous Vehicles: State Tort Liability, Automobile Insurance, and Federal Safety Regulation," *California Law Rev*iew, Vol. 105, No. 6, 2017, pp. 1611–1694.

*General Motors Corp. v. Johnston*, 592 So. 2d 1054, Ala., 1992.

Gerla, M., E.-K. Lee, G. Pau, and U. Lee, "Internet of Vehicles: From Intelligent Grid to Autonomous Cars and Vehicular Clouds," *IEEE World Forum on Internet of Things (WF-IoT)*, Seoul, South Korea, 2014, pp. 241–246.

Glancy, D., "Privacy in Autonomous Vehicles," *Santa Clara Law Review*, Vol. 52, No. 4, 2012, pp. 1171–1239.

Glancy, D., "Autonomous and Automated and Connected Cars—Oh My: First Generation Autonomous Cars in the Legal Ecosystem," *Minnesota Journal of Law, Science, and Technology*, Vol. 16, No. 2, 2015, pp. 619–691.

Glancy, D., R. Peterson, and K. F. Graham, "A Look at the Legal Environment for Driverless Vehicles," *Legal Research Digest*, Vol. 69, 2016.

Goodin, D., "White House Fails to Make Case That Russian Hackers Tampered with Election," *ARS Technica*, December 30, 2016. As of June 23, 2017: https://arstechnica.com/security/2016/12/did-russia-tamper-with-the-2016-election-bitter-debate-likely-to-rage-on/

Gopalakrishnan, R., and M. Mogato, "Bangladesh Bank Official's Computer Was Hacked to Carry Out $81 Million Heist: Diplomat," Reuters, May 19, 2016. As of June 23, 2017: http://www.reuters.com/article/us-cyber-heist-philippines-idUSKCN0YA0CH

Graham, K., "Of Frightened Horses and Autonomous Vehicles: Tort Law and Its Assimilation of Innovations," *Santa Clara Law Review*, Vol. 52, 2012, pp. 101–131.

Grande, A., "Adobe to Settle Data Breach Claims Over 3M Payment Cards," *Law 360*, April 23, 2015. As of July 3, 2018: http://www.law360.com/articles/647097/adobe-to-settle-data-breach-claims-over-3m-payment-cards

Greenberg, A., "Radio Attack Lets Hackers Steal 24 Different Car Models," *Wired*, March 21, 2016a. As of June 23, 2017:
https://www.wired.com/2016/03/
study-finds-24-car-models-open-unlocking-ignition-hack/

Greenberg, A., "A New Wireless Hack Can Unlock 100 Million Volkswagens," *Wired*, August 10, 2016b. As of June 23, 2017:
https://www.wired.com/2016/08/
oh-good-new-hack-can-unlock-100-million-volkswagens/

Grushkin, D., "Cargo Theft: The New Highway Robbery," *Bloomberg Businessweek*, May 26, 2011. As of June 23, 2017:
https://www.bloomberg.com/news/articles/2011-05-26/
cargo-theft-the-new-highway-robbery

Gurney, J., "Sue My Car Not Me: Products Liability and Accidents Involving Autonomous Vehicles," *University of Illinois Journal of Law, Technology, and Policy*, Vol. 247, 2013.

Gurney, J., "Driving into the Unknown: Examining the Crossroads of Criminal Law and Autonomous Vehicles," *Wake Forest Journal of Law and Policy*, Vol. 393, 2015.

Gutierrez, G., and P. Helsel, "North Carolina 'Can Opener' Bridge Continues to Wreak Havoc on Trucks," *NBC News*, January 7, 2016. As of June 23, 2017:
http://www.nbcnews.com/nightly-news/
north-carolina-can-opener-bridge-continues-wreak-havoc-trucks-n492511

*Hasson v. Ford Motor Co.*, 650 P.2d 1171, Cal., 1982.

*Helene Cahen et al. v. Toyota Motor Corporation et al.*, case no. 3:15-cv-01104, U.S. District Court for the Northern District of California, First Amended Complaint.

Herridge, C., and L. Tomlinson, "Terror Fiend Tricked Police to Get Death Truck Onto Busy Nice Promenade, Kill 84," *Fox News World*, July 15, 2016. As of June 23, 2017:
http://www.foxnews.com/world/2016/07/15/
at-least-80-dead-18-seriously-injured-in-bastille-day-terror-attack-in-france.html

Hubbard, F., "'Sophisticated Robots': Balancing Liability, Regulation, and Innovation," *Florida Law Review*, Vol. 66, No. 5, 2014, pp. 1803–1872.

*In re Air Crash Near Cali, Colombia on December 20, 1995*, 985 F. Supp. 1106, S.D. Fla, 1997.

International Association of Lemon Law Administrators, "Publications," last updated May 2018. As of June 18, 2019:
http://www.ialla.net/pub_1.htm

Jacobson, M., and M. Wetzel, "Security Weaknesses in Bluetooth," *Topics in Cryptology*, CT-RSA, 2001, pp. 176–191.

Johnson, Vincent R., "The Boundary-Line Function of the Economic Loss Rule," *Washington & Lee Law Review*, Vol. 66, 2009, pp. 523–585.

Kalra, Nidhi, James M. Anderson, and Martin Wachs, *Liability and Regulation of Autonomous Vehicle Technologies*, Berkeley, Calif.: California PATH Program, Institute of Transportation Studies, University of California at Berkeley, 2009. As of May 7, 2019:
https://www.rand.org/pubs/external_publications/EP20090427.html

Kato, S., S. Tsugawa, K. Tokuda, T. Matsui, and H. Fujii, "Vehicle Control Algorithms for Cooperative Driving with Automated Vehicles and Intervehicle Communications," *Intelligent Transportation Systems, IEEE Transactions*, Vol. 3, No. 3, 2002, pp. 115–161.

*Kawananakoa v. Polyblank*, 205 U.S. 349, 1907.

Keen Security Lab of Tencent, "Car Hacking Research: Remote Attack Tesla Motors," *Keen Security Lab Blog*, September 19, 2016. As of June 23, 2017:
http://keenlab.tencent.com/en/2016/09/19/
Keen-Security-Lab-of-Tencent-Car-Hacking-Research-Remote-Attack-to-Tesla-Cars/

Kelion, L., "Nissan Disables Leaf App After Car Hack Risk Revealed Online," *BBC News*, February 25, 2016. As of June 23, 2017:
http://www.bbc.com/news/technology-35660641

Kohler, W., and A. Colbert-Taylor, "Current Law and Potential Legal Issues Pertaining to Automated, Autonomous and Connected Vehicles," *Santa Clara High Technology Law Journal*, Vol. 31, 2014.

Korosec, K., "Volvo CEO: We Will Accept All Liability When Our Cars Are in Autonomous Mode," *Fortune*, 2015. As of July 2, 2018:
http://fortune.com/2015/10/07/volvo-liability-self-driving-cars

Koscher, K., A. Czeskis, F. Roesner, S. Patel, and T. Kohno, "Experimental Security Analysis of a Modern Automobile," *IEEE Symposium on Security and Privacy*, 2010, pp. 447–462.

Krauss, M., "Public Services Meet Private Law," *San Diego Law Review*, Vol. 43, No. 1, 2007.

Kravets, D., "WI-FI–Hacking Neighbor from Hell Sentenced to 18 Years," *Wired*, July 12, 2011. As of June 23, 2017:
https://www.wired.com/2011/07/hacking-neighbor-from-hell/

*Krider Pharmacy & Gifts, Inc. v. Medi-Care Data Sys., Inc.*, 791 F. Supp. 221, E.D. Wis., 1992.

Kuchler, H., "Cyber Security Alert on Qualcomm's Android Chips," *Financial Times*, August 7, 2016. As of August 15, 2016:
http://www.ft.com/cms/s/0/11b8cabe-5c7c-11e6-a72a-bd4bf1198c63.html

*Laurence v. United States*, 851 F. Supp. 1445, N.D. Cal., 1994.

Laurendeau, C., and M. Barbeau, "Threats to Security in DSRC/WAVE," *International Conference on Ad-Hoc Networks and Wireless*, Berlin, Heidelberg: Springer, 2006, pp. 266–279.

Lee, B.-H., S.-H. An, and D.-R. Shin, "A Remote Control Service for OSGi-Based Unmanned Vehicle Using Smartphone in Ubiquitous Environment," *CICSyN 2011: Third International Conference on Computational Intelligence, Communication Systems and Networks,* Bali, Indonesia, 2011, pp. 158–163. As of June 22, 2017: http://ieeexplore.ieee.org/xpl/mostRecentIssue.jsp?punumber=6005193

Lendon, B., "SUV Flees Cops, Takes Out Navy Fighter Jet," *CNN*, April 1, 2016. As of June 23, 2017:
http://www.cnn.com/2016/04/01/politics/suv-crashes-into-navy-f-a-18-fighter-jet/

Levin, S., "Witness Says Self-Driving Uber Ran Red Light on Its Own, Disputing Uber's Claims," *The Guardian*, December 21, 2016. As of June 23, 2017:
https://www.theguardian.com/technology/2016/dec/21/
witness-says-self-driving-uber-ran-red-light-on-its-own-disputing-ubers-claims

*Lewis v. United States Navy*, 865 F. Supp. 294, D.S.C., 1994.

Li, Y., "An Overview of the DSRC/WAVE Technology," *International Conference on Heterogeneous Networking for Quality, Reliability, Security and Robustness*, Berlin, Heidelberg: Springer, 2010, pp. 544–558.

*Lille v. Thompson*, 332 U.S. 459, 1947.

Lilley, Stephen, Jonathan Weinberg, and Archis A. Parasharami, "New California Consumer Privacy Act Increases the Risk of Additional Data Breach Class Actions," *Mayer Brown Class Defense Blog*, July 19, 2018. As of June 18, 2019:
https://www.classdefenseblog.com/2018/07/
new-california-consumer-privacy-act-increases-risk-additional-data-breach-class-actions/

Loukas, G., "Chapter 7: Physical-Cyber Attacks," in T. Stover, ed., *Cyber-Physical Attacks: A Growing Invisible Threat*, Oxford, UK: Butterworth-Heinemann, pp. 221–253.

Magnusen, J., "Target Corporation Customer MDL No. 14-2522 (PAM/JJK) Data Security Breach Litigation," 2014. As of July 2, 2018:
http://www.kslaw.com/library/newsletters/dataprivacysecurity/2014/1222/
dps122214_TargetConsumerMTDOrder.pdf

Magnuson-Moss Warranty Act, 15 U.S.C. §§ 2301–2312, 2012.

Marchant, G., and R. Lindor, "The Coming Collision Between Autonomous Vehicles and the Liability System," *Santa Clara Law Review*, Vol. 52, No. 4, 2012, pp. 1321–1340.

Marmouyet, F., "French State Faces Lawsuits Over Failure to Thwart Terrorist Attacks," *France 24*, July 22, 2016. As of June 23, 2017:
http://www.france24.com/en/
20160722-french-state-lawsuits-terrorist-attacks-nice-mohamed-lahouaiej-bouhlel

Marr, Bernard, "GDPR: The Biggest Data Breaches and the Shocking Fines (That Would Have Been)," Forbes.com, June 11, 2018. As of June 18, 2019:
https://www.forbes.com/sites/bernardmarr/2018/06/11/
gdpr-the-biggest-data-breaches-and-the-shocking-fines-that-would-have-been/
#7a4e51fe6c10

Marshall, Aarian, and Alex Davies, "Uber's Self-Driving Car Saw the Woman It Killed," *Wired*, May 24, 2018. As of June 30, 2019:
https://www.wired.com/story/uber-self-driving-crash-arizona-ntsb-report/

McGinty, K., "Consumer Claims Survive Motion to Dismiss in Target Data Breach Class Act," *Martindale*, 2015. As of June 17, 2019:
http://www.martindale.com/litigation-law/
article_Mintz-Levin-Cohn-Ferris-Glovsky-Popeo-PC_2195720.htm

McNicholas, E., V. Mohan, C. Northouse, and K. Frumkin, *Cybersecurity: A Practical Guide to the Law of Cyber Risk*, Practicing Law Institute, 2015.

Mele, D., "The Quasi-Autonomous Car as an Assistive Device for Blind Drivers: Overcoming Liability and Regulatory Barriers," *Syracuse Journal of Science and Technology Law Reporter*, Vol. 28, 2013, pp. 26–64.

Miller, C., and C. Valasek, "A Survey of Remote Automotive Attack Surfaces," undated. As of August 4, 2016:
https://sm.asisonline.org/
ASIS%20SM%20Documents/remote%20attack%20surfaces.pdf

Montgomery, J., "I-495 Bridge Damage: Delaware Tries to Recover Costs," *Delaware Online*, April 15, 2015. As of June 23, 2017:
http://www.delawareonline.com/story/news/local/2015/04/15/
bridge-legal/25849097/

*Morden v. Cont. AG*, 611 N.W.2d 659, Wis., 2000.

Mueller, B., W. Rashbaum, and A. Baker, "Terror Attack Kills 8 and Injures 11 in Manhattan," *New York Times*, October 31, 2017. As of June 19, 2018:
https://www.nytimes.com/2017/10/31/nyregion/
police-shooting-lower-manhattan.html?_r=0

Musk, E., "A Most Peculiar Test Drive," *Tesla Blog*, February 13, 2013. As of June 23, 2017:
https://www.tesla.com/blog/most-peculiar-test-drive

National Conference of State Legislatures, "Autonomous Vehicle State Bill Tracking Database," 2018. As of June 17, 2019:
http://www.ncsl.org/research/transportation/autonomous-vehicles-legislative-database.aspx

National Highway Traffic Safety Administration, "Cybersecurity Best Practices for Modern Vehicles. (Report No. DOT HS 812 333)," 2016a. As of June 23, 2017:
https://www.nhtsa.gov/staticfiles/nvs/pdf/812333_CybersecurityForModernVehicles.pdf

National Highway Traffic Safety Administration, "New Manufacturers Handbook: Requirements for Manufacturers of Motor Vehicles and Motor Vehicle Equipment," 2016b. As of June 29, 2018:
https://vpic.nhtsa.dot.gov/Manufacturer_Handbook_20161019.pdf

National Institute of Standards and Technology, *Risk Management Framework for Information Systems and Organizations: A System Life Cycle Approach for Security and Privacy (12/20/18) SP 800-37 Rev. 2 (DOI)*, Gaithersburg, Md., 2018.

National Institute of Standards and Technology and CPS Public Working Group, "CPS PWG Cyber-Physical Systems (CPS) Framework Release 1.0," 2017. As of June 23, 2017:
https://pages.nist.gov/cpspwg/

Neuburger, J., and M. Garde, "Information Security Vulnerabilities: Should We Litigate or Mitigate?" *Software Law Bulletin*, 2004.

*Ngiraingas v. Sanchez*, 495 U.S. 182, 1998.

NHSTA—*See* National Highway Traffic Safety Administration.

NIST—*See* National Institute of Standards and Technology.

O'Connell, P., K. Thayer, and J. Panzar, "Organized 'Crash-and-Grab' Burglaries Using Vehicles Plague Chicago," *Los Angeles Times*, January 3, 2015. As of June 23, 2017:
http://www.latimes.com/nation/la-na-crash-and-grab-20150104-story.html

Ondrovic, R., "Municipal Tort Liability for Criminal Attacks Against Passengers on Mass Transportation," *Fordham Urban Law Journal*, Vol. 12, No. 2, 1983, pp. 325–348.

Owen, D., "Proving Negligence in Modern Products Liability Litigation," *Arizona State Law Journal*, Vol. 36, 2004, pp. 1003–1038.

Pagliery, J., "The Inside Story of the Biggest Hack in History," *CNN Tech*, August 5, 2015. As of June 23, 2017:
http://money.cnn.com/2015/08/05/technology/aramco-hack/

Petit, J., and S. Shladover, "Potential Cyberattacks on Automated Vehicles," *Intelligent Transportation Systems, IEEE Transactions,* Vol. 16, No. 2, 2015, pp. 546–556.

Pleskot, K., "ISIS Working on Weaponizing Self-Driving Cars, NATO Expert Warns," *MotorTrend*, May 2, 2016. As of June 23, 2017:
http://www.motortrend.com/news/isis-working-on-weaponizing-self-driving-cars-nato-expert-warns/

Porges, S., "How to Design a New Car in 7 Steps," *Forbes*, December 6, 2015. As of June 29, 2018:
https://www.forbes.com/sites/sethporges/2015/12/06/these-are-the-7-steps-it-takes-to-design-a-new-auto-product/#13fdb248517a

Privacy Act of 1974, H.R. Rep. No. 89-1919, 1966.

Prosser, W. L., and W. P. Keeton, *Torts*, 5th ed., St. Paul, Minn.: West Group, 1984.

"Ram-Raid Gang Steals Cash Machine," *BBC News*, March 19, 2007. As of June 23, 2017:
http://news.bbc.co.uk/2/hi/uk_news/england/west_yorkshire/6467475.stm

Rana, R., M. Staron, J. Hansson, and M. Nilsson, "Defect Prediction Over Software Life Cycle in Automotive Domain State of the Art and Road Map for Future," paper presented at 9th International Conference on Software Engineering and Applications (ICSOFT-EA 2014), 2014.

Reiter, R., "Gone in 60 Seconds: ATM 'Crash and Grab' Crime on the Rise," *ATM Marketplace*, April 17, 2014. As of June 23, 2017:
https://www.atmmarketplace.com/articles/gone-in-60-seconds-atm-crash-and-grab-crime-on-the-rise/

Restatement (Second) of Torts § 402A, American Law Institute, 1965.

Restatement (Second) of Torts § 895B, American Law Institute, 1979.

Restatement (Third) of Torts: § 5, American Law Institute, 2000.

Restatement (Third) of Torts: Apportionment Liability § 8, American Law Institute, 2000.

Restatement (Third) of Torts: Prods. Liab. § 2, American Law Institute, 2000.

Restatement (Third) of Torts: Prods. Liab. § 21, American Law Institute, 2000.

Riley, M., B. Elgin, D. Lawrence, and C. Matlack, "Missed Alarms and 40 Million Stolen Credit Card Numbers: How Target Blew It," *Bloomberg*, 2014. As of June 19, 2018:
https://www.bloomberg.com/news/articles/2014-03-13/target-missed-warnings-in-epic-hack-of-credit-card-data

Ring, T., "Connected Cars–The Next Target for Hackers," *Network Security*, Vol. 11, 2015, pp. 11–16.

Risen, T., "How Safe Is a Self-Driving Car?" *U.S. News and World Report*, 2015. As of July 2, 2018:
http://www.usnews.com/news/articles/2015/10/08/nhtsa-volvo-seek-cybersecurity-privacy-for-driverless-cars

Roberts, S., A. Hightower, M. Thornton, L. Cunningham, and R. Terry, *Advanced Vehicle Control Systems: Potential Tort Liability for Developers*, San Francisco, Calif.: Nossaman, Guthner, Knox, and Elliott, 1993.

Rojas, C., "N.J. Mayor Vows to Sue Amazon Over Warehouse Traffic Gridlock," *NJ.com*, December 2, 2015. As of June 23, 2017:
http://www.nj.com/mercer/index.ssf/2015/12/nj_mayor_vows_to_sue_amazon_over_warehouse_traffic.html

Root, K., "Albuquerque Citizens, Business Owners Sue City Over ART Project," *KRQE News 13*, April 4, 2016.

Ropes & Gray, "Potential Implications of Supreme Court's Decision in Carpenter v. United States," Lexology Newsfeed, July 6, 2018. As of June 18, 2019:
https://www.lexology.com/library/detail.aspx?g=f5e6800a-d1fa-4534-8afa-d85aa1c3455c

Royal Academy of Engineering, *Smart Infrastructure: The Future*, London, England: The Royal Academy of Engineering, 2012. As of May 1, 2016:
http://www.raeng.org.uk/publications/reports/smart-infrastructure-the-future

Rubin, J., D. Briscoe, and M. Landsberg, "Car Plows Through Crowd in Santa Monica, Killing 9," *Los Angeles Times*, July 17, 2003. As of June 23, 2017:
http://articles.latimes.com/2003/jul/17/local/me-smcrash17

Rustad, Michael L., and Thomas H. Koenig, "The Tort of Negligent Enablement of Cybercrime," *Berkeley Technology Law Journal*, Vol. 20, No. 4, 2005, pp. 1553–1611.

SAE International, "SAE J3061 Cybersecurity Guidebook for Cyber-Physical Vehicle Systems," briefing, undated. As of June 19, 2018:
https://interact.gsa.gov/sites/default/files/J3061%20JP%20presentation.pdf

Sampath, A., H. Dai, H. Zheng, and B. Zhao, "Multi-Channel Jamming Attacks Using Cognitive Radios," *Proceedings of the 16th International Conference on Computer Communications and Networks*, 2007, pp. 352–357.

Sawaya, D., "Not Just for Products Liability: Applying the Economic Loss Rule Beyond Its Origins," *Fordham Law Review*, Vol. 83, No. 2, 2014, pp. 1073–1106.

Scott, M., "Tort Liability for Vendors of Insecure Software: Has the Time Finally Come?" *Maryland Law Review*, Vol. 67, No. 2, 2008, pp. 425–484.

Shipeng, G., "Sulphuric Acid Spill Pollutes China River," Reuters, February 12, 2008. As of June 23, 2017:
http://www.reuters.com/article/environment-china-accident-dc-idUSPEK27254020080213

Sitawarin, Chawin, Arjun Nitin Bhagoji, Arsalan Mosenia, Mung Chiang, and Prateek Mittal, "DARTS: Deceiving Autonomous Cars with Toxic Signs," *Association for Computing Machinery*, May 2018. As of April 30, 2019: https://arxiv.org/pdf/1802.06430.pdf

Smith, B., "Proximity-Driven Liability," *Georgetown Law Journal*, Vol. 102, November 1, 2013, pp. 1777–1820.

SRI International, "DHS Programs: Cybersecurity for Government Vehicles," paper presented at Annual Computer Security Applications Conference, 2015. As of June 17, 2019:
https://www.acsac.org/2015/program/ACSAC%202015%20Vehicle%20Cybersecurity%20-%20Balenson.pdf

*Stansbie v. Troman*, 2 K.B. 48, 1948.

Steinhauer, J., M. Mazzetti, and J. Hirschfeld Davis, "Congress Votes to Override Obama Veto on 9/11 Victims Bill," *New York Times*, September 28, 2016. As of June 23, 2017:
http://www.nytimes.com/2016/09/29/us/politics/senate-votes-to-override-obama-veto-on-9-11-victims-bill.html?_r=0

Stock, S., L. Wagner, and F. Escamilla, "Pirates on the Highways: Cargo Theft Costing Nation Billions," *NBC News*, August 5, 2012. As of June 23, 2017: https://usnews.newsvine.com/_news/2012/08/05/13132047-pirates-on-the-highways-cargo-theft-costing-nation-billions

Streck, S., "Supreme Court Rejects Business's Loss of Value Claim for Lost Street Access," *The Preeminent Domain*, January 15, 2015. As of June 23, 2017: http://thepreeminentdomain.com/supreme-court-rejects-businesss-loss-of-value-claim-for-lost-street-access/

*Sturbridge Partners Ltd. v. Walker*, 482 S.E.2d 339, Ga., 1997.

Sturgeon, M., "Update: Power Restored After Crash Causes Outage," *KMTV 3 News Now*, January 25, 2016. As of June 23, 2017:
http://www.3newsnow.com/news/local-news/oppd-3k-without-power-after-delivery-truck-crash

Su, W., H. Eichi, W. Zeng, and M.-Y. Chow, "A Survey on the Electrification of Transportation in a Smart Grid Environment," *Industrial Informatics, IEEE Transactions*, Vol. 8, No. 1, 2012, pp. 1–10.

Sumra, I. A., I. Ahmad, H. Hasbullah, and J.-L. bin Ab Manan. "Classes of Attacks in VANET," *2011 Saudi International Electronics, Communications and Photonics Conference (SIECPC)*, 2011, pp. 1–5.

Sundvall, S., and M. Andolina, "The Status of Pending Air Carrier Litigation," *Journal of Air Law and Commerce*, Vol. 66, No. 1, 2000, pp. 167–222.

Swanson, A., "'Somebody Grab the Wheel!': State Autonomous Vehicle Legislation and the Road to a National Regime," *Marquette Law Review*, Vol. 97, No. 4, 2014, pp. 1087–1147.

Szwed, R., "Disabling System for a Vehicle," U.S. Patent 5,861,799, issued January 19, 1999.

*Tafuri v. Jeppesen Sanderson, Inc.*, 25 F. Supp. 2d 1364, Dist. Court, S.D. Fla., 1998.

"Truck with Missiles Crashes in Louisiana," *New York Times*, January 2, 1993. As of June 23, 2017:
http://www.nytimes.com/1993/01/02/us/truck-with-missiles-crashes-in-louisiana.html

Tuck, S., "To the Rescue: Liability in Negligence for Third Party Criminal Acts in the United States and Australia," *Indiana International and Comparative Law Review*, Vol. 23, No. 2, 2013.

Uniform Commercial Code § 2-714(2).

U.S. Department of Homeland Security, "Critical Infrastructure Sectors," December 30, 2016. As of June 23, 2017:
https://www.dhs.gov/critical-infrastructure-sectors

U.S. Department of Homeland Security, "Commercial Facilities Sector," June 13, 2017. As of June 23, 2017:
https://www.dhs.gov/commercial-facilities-sector

U.S. Department of Homeland Security, "Snapshot: DHS, DOT Partner on Government Vehicle Telematics Cybersecurity Primer," May 15, 2018. As of June 18, 2019:
https://www.dhs.gov/science-and-technology/news/2018/05/15/snapshot-dhs-dot-partner-government-vehicle-telematics

U.S. Department of Transportation, *Automated Vehicles Policy: Accelerating the Next Revolution in Roadway Safety*, September 21, 2016. As of June 2, 2018:
https://www.transportation.gov/sites/dot.gov/files/docs/AV%20policy%20guidance%20PDF.pdf

U.S. Department of Transportation, *Automated Driving Systems 2.0: A Vision for Safety*, September 2017. As of June 30, 2019:
https://www.nhtsa.gov/sites/nhtsa.dot.gov/files/documents/13069a-ads2.0_090617_v9a_tag.pdf

U.S. Department of Transportation, *Preparing for the Future of Transportation: Automated Vehicles 3.0*, October 4, 2018. As of June 30, 2019:
https://www.transportation.gov/sites/dot.gov/files/docs/policy-initiatives/automated-vehicles/320711/preparing-future-transportation-automated-vehicle-30.pdf

Viereckl, R., D. Ahlemann, A. Koster, E. Hirsh, F. Kuhnert, J. Mohs, M. Fischer, W. Gerling, K. Gnanasekaran, J. Kusber, J. Stephan, D. Crusius, H. Kerstan, T. Warnke, M. Schulte, J. Seyfferth, and E. H. Baker, "Connected Car Report 2016: Opportunities, Risk, and Turmoil on the Road to Autonomous Vehicles," *Strategy&*, September 28, 2016. As of July 3, 2018: https://www.strategyand.pwc.com/report/connected-car-2016-study

Villasenor, J., *Products Liability and Driverless Cars: Issues and Guiding Principles for Legislation*, Vol. 2, Washington, D.C.: Brookings Institution, 2014.

Virginia Transportation Research Council, "Tort Liability: A Handbook for Employees of the Virginia Department of Transportation and Virginia Municipal Corporations," Charlottesville, Va., 2004. As of July 2, 2018: http://www.virginiadot.org/vtrc/main/online_reports/pdf/04-r30.pdf

Vladeck, D., "Machines Without Principals: Liability Rules and Artificial Intelligence," *Washington Law Review*, Vol. 89, 2014, pp. 117–150.

Weiner, G., and B. W. Smith, "Automated Driving: Legislative and Regulatory Action," Stanford, Calif.: Center for Internet and Society, Stanford University, April 27, 2017. As of June 17, 2019: http://cyberlaw.stanford.edu/wiki/index.php/Automated_Driving:_Legislative_and_Regulatory_Action

Weise, E., "Check If You Were Hit by the Massive 'Avalanche' Cybercrime Ring," *USA Today*, December 2, 2016. As of June 23, 2017: https://www.usatoday.com/story/tech/news/2016/12/02/massive-180-country-cybercrime-bust-avalanche-group-interpol-fbi/94811966/

Whittaker, Z., "'Quadrooter' Flaws Affect Over 900 Million Android Phones," *Zero Day*, August 7, 2016. As of June 19, 2018: http://www.zdnet.com/article/quadrooter-security-flaws-affect-over-900-million-android-phones/

Wiedeman, R., "The Big Hack: The Day Cars Drove Themselves into Walls and the Hospitals Froze," *New York Magazine*, June 19, 2016. As of June 23, 2017: http://nymag.com/daily/intelligencer/2016/06/the-hack-that-could-take-down-nyc.html

Williams, Claire, "Self-Driving Cars and 'Safety-Critical' Software Updates," *Mills & Reeve: Technology Law Update*, October 30, 2017. As of June 18, 2019: http://www.technology-law-blog.co.uk/2017/10/self-driving-cars-and-safety-critical-software-updates.html

Williams, D., "Relatives of Palestinian Attack Victims Sue Facebook for $1 Billion in U.S.," Reuters, July 11, 2016. As of June 23, 2017: http://www.reuters.com/article/us-israel-palestinians-facebook-idUSKCN0ZR1G0

Wiretap Act, 18 U.S.C. § 2511, 1968.

Wittenberg, S., "Automated Vehicles: Strict Products Liability, Negligence Liability and Proliferation," *Illinois Business Law Journal*, January 7, 2016. As of June 19, 2019:
https://publish.illinois.edu/illinoisblj/2016/01/07/automated-vehicles-strict-products-liability-negligence-liability-and-proliferation/

Woolley, S., "Equifax's Massive Hack Has a Tiny Silver Lining," *Bloomberg*, September 25, 2017. As of June 19, 2018:
https://www.bloomberg.com/news/articles/2017-09-25/equifax-s-massive-hack-has-a-tiny-silver-lining

Wright, A., "Hacking Cars," *Communications of the ACM*, Vol. 54, No. 11, November 2011, pp. 18–19.

Wu, S., "Product Liability Issues in the U.S. and Associated Risk Management," in M. Maurer, J. Gerdes, B. Lenz, and H. Winner, eds., *Autonomes Fahren*, Berlin, Heidelberg: Springer, 2015, pp. 575–592.

Wyglinski, A., X. Huang, T. Padir, L. Lai, T. Eisenbarth, and K. Venkatasubramanian, "Security of Autonomous Systems Employing Embedded Computing and Sensors," *Micro-IEEE*, Vol. 33, No. 1, 2013, pp. 80–86.

Yadron, D., and D. Tynan, "Tesla Driver Dies in First Fatal Crash While Using Autopilot Mode," *The Guardian*, June 30, 2016. As of June 23, 2017:
https://www.theguardian.com/technology/2016/jun/30/tesla-autopilot-death-self-driving-car-elon-musk

Yağdereli, E., C. Gemci, and A. Aktaş, "A Study on Cyber-Security of Autonomous and Unmanned Vehicles," *Journal of Defense Modeling and Simulation: Applications, Methodology, Technology*, Vol. 12, No. 4, 2015, pp. 369–381.

You, S., M. Krage, and L. Jalics, "Overview of Remote Diagnosis and Maintenance for Automotive Systems," *SAE Technical Paper*, 2005, pp. 1–8.

# About the Authors

**Zev Winkelman** is an information scientist at the RAND Corporation specializing in big data analytics, social media, and cyber security. His interests include research in defense, intelligence, foreign policy, law enforcement, economic and health. He has a Ph.D. in public policy and an M.S. in forensic computing and counterterrorism.

**Maya Buenaventura** is the research manager at the California Policy Lab. Her interests include criminal justice policy, program evaluation, empirical legal studies, immigration and border enforcement, health care, legislation of technology and cyberspace, and alternative dispute resolution and law reform. She has a Ph.D. in public policy, a J.D., and a B.A. in economics.

**James M. Anderson** is a senior behavioral/social scientist at the RAND Corporation and the director of the Justice Policy Program and the RAND Institute for Civil Justice. His research focuses on civil and criminal justice. He has led projects on forensic science, indigent defense, and the policy implications of autonomous vehicles. He holds a J.D. and a B.A. in ethics, politics, and economics.

**Nahom M. Beyene** is an engineer at the RAND Corporation. His interests include the intersection of technology and transportation policy, the balance of safety and security, human factors with robotics and automation, and information assurance with cyber security risks.

He has a Ph.D. in rehabilitation science, an M.S. in biomechanical engineering, and a B.S. in mechanical engineering.

**Pavan Katkar** is an assistant policy researcher at the RAND Corporation. His research focuses on issues at the intersection of technology and policy. He holds an M.A. in science and security and a B.S. in engineering in the field of information science.

**Gregory Cyril Baumann** is the manager of the Research Communications Group at the RAND Corporation. He has a J.D. and a B.A. in rhetoric.